Letting Go

Letting Go

Andrea Cottrell

Rev. date: 03/02/2017

To order additional copies of this book, contact:
Xlibris
1-888-795-4274
www.Xlibris.com
Orders@Xlibris.com
756882

To God and all lost souls.

Table of Contents

Chapter 1 THE YEAR IT ALL BEGAN

This was the year it all begins, as many people say the best four years of your life. I always get excited for the first day back to school. It's a time to start over, to do better than the previous year, a time to make more memories and new friends, or even catch up with old friends you haven't seen all summer. At least that's what I use to think. Many things changed freshman year. As I pushed open the doors of Lampade High School, the stench of overdramatic teens with cocky attitudes filled the air. There's something about highschool that makes teens act like they're either immature and belong in middle school or it makes them think they're too mature and they act like their twenty.

I made my way to my locker where I was greeted by my friends. We chatted some time before the warning bell rung. I was now sitting in first period, trying to focus in on the teacher talking about what we will learn during our time in class. The day went on, just like any other ordinary day. Finally I walked into last period, Ms. Frans class. What I would soon find out is that this class and this specific teacher would be of great importance to my life and journey throughout high school.

As the days got longer, classes dragged on and everyone started to get into their normal routine. It seemed as though the year was going to be like any other. We didn't know exactly what this year had in store. We as a community didn't know how this year would change us as a whole and individually until September 27th came along.

It was a Sunday afternoon and I had just woken up from a nap. Immediately I checked my phone, scrolled through my messages, Facebook and then Instagram. I found out Jake Mallen, a student enrolled at Lampade high school had passed away in a plane crash and boy did this take its toll on every breathing individual in the community of Lampade. His last week on earth, I saw him often and talked very little. You could spot his smile from miles away. There was something unique about Jake that was easily sensed in his presence. He was one of those light up the room when they make an entrance type.

The following Monday I witnessed something unforgettable. As soon as I walked down freshman hall, I felt the instant sensation of the pain that lived and breathed through the hallways. In every direction there was students crying and comforting one another. During this week I also gave and received comfort. This had an impact on me as I'm sure it did every other student.

In some ways this tragic occurrence had brought the Lampade community closer. Although the pain got easier to tolerate, the memory of Jake and that day, never faded away. What we didn't know was that this was only the beginning. That was one of three that passed during my freshman year at Lampade high school. Hailey Hones, a kind-hearted young girl, had also passed. Although she hadn't made her way to highschool yet, the effects of the tragedy made it's way to all of us. It was hard to know that a peer had taken her own life because of how badly she was treated by others.

It brought attention to the subject and made us all react. Mrs. Embead, who was fighting a long battle of cancer, also passed shortly after. Each of theses deaths have taken it's toll on Lampade. These deaths had influenced the way everyone lived the rest of their lives. We all appreciated life more than ever the following months to come. The worst part is, this was just the beginning for me. As everyone started to get back into their normal routines, the year had finally began. Homework, essays, tests, you name it, we got it. The only stress free days were the weekends. Hockey time. I love hockey, especially the people I've met though it. Coach being one of those people.

Her driven passion for the sport inspired me to work hard. There was something different about her, She has stars in her eyes. When I first joined her team in 7th grade, I felt like I was in the presence of a legend. Although I still feel that way, there's much more to her than that. I loved coming to her practices, I learned more from her than I did from any other coach (I would meet in the future.) The ice is my happy place. As soon as I stepped on the ice, all my worries would disappear.

Sports offers much more than what the eye can see. A team becomes a family, a person becomes a player, a coach becomes a teacher. There's so much untapped potential and hidden talent. Sports offer teens a chance to show what they've got and use teamwork to build a wider horizon for themselves.

It was the weekend after Jakes death, and I still managed to make it to hockey. I had notified Coach because I didn't want her to think that I wasn't giving my hundred percent for nothing. When I walked into the locker room, I threw down my bag and plugged in my headphones. As I was tying my skates, Coach came over and sat down next to me.

Ignoring her, I continued until she stopped me. I unplugged one headphone out of my ear and she gave me a hug, which is very unusual for her. She's the type you have to peel back a layer at a time and I had only just begun trying to find out what laid inside the tough exterior of hers. When she hugged me, I tried so hard to hold back the tears but no matter what they were coming. She whispered, so gently, "I'll let go when you want me to." I squeezed a little harder and then with a slow motion, I let go. I finished putting on my gear and walked out the door. I stepped on the ice and like magic, my tears dried and I cleared my mind. When I walked out after practice that day, I knew I had just gained a lifetime Coach and friend. I will never forget those words.

I went home and took a good look at my life. I noticed how much my appreciation for Hockey had grown drastically over the past few months. Hockey has helped me relieve stress and pain in ways I can't believe. Just being in the presence of a team working hard to perfect their crafts has taught me a lot about what it means to be a hockey player. Hockey has done so much for me. After a short weekend, it was time to return to school. During this time along with all the tragedies at Lampade, I had some troubles of my own. I had just started to date an old friend. I guess he's always had a crush on me and I never really figured it out. He, whom shall not be named, was that kid your parents warned you about. He was into drugs and his grades weren't the best. He definitely wasn't someone I would go for but after much thought, I decided that maybe he just needs someone to help him change and it couldn't hurt to try.

We were about a month into our relationship. We must've went on about five dates. Everything was going well until he showed his true colors. It was a Thursday night and we were in his room talking about boxing. I began to joke around saying I could totally beat him up if I tried. Which maybe I could have, until it got serious.

We began to jokingly fight. Then, he slapped me in the face. I went from laughing to a more serious tone. I recall saying "I was just kidding, we're not actually hitting" and as the tone in his voice changed, he replied "you can handle it" as he did it once more. I then took a seat on his bed, not amused and utterly annoyed. My mom had pulled in to pick me up and he walked me out. After that I didn't think much of it, until it got worse.

A few days later, he saw me in the hallway. I was going one way and he was going another. He quickly grabbed my arm and pulled hard. It was so fast I felt like I had whiplash and hit the person behind me. I walked to the side of the hallway where he met me. As I was breathing faster than usual, he looked at me in a confused way and said "alright well I'll see you later" as if nothing just happened. I thought to myself, what was the purpose of doing that if he just wanted to say hi.

Later that day I was waiting for my friend to walk to my next class and he passed by shoving me into my locker. I was caught off guard and went straight into my locker. This continued on for quite sometime, as time went on he yelled at me for things that weren't of my doing and he pushed, tripped and kicked me. Sometimes, marks would even show up.

Then one day, my friend and I were talking at my locker when he came to join, we had to leave or else we would be late. I told him, "I have to go, the bell is going to ring" he grabbed my arm and said "I wasn't done talking to you." I kept trying to pull away until he finally let go. My friend had said in a worried tone "are you okay?" I replied in an unsure tone "yeah, I'm fine why?" She looked at me, with her eyebrows scrunched and her eyes piercing in on mine, as if she didn't believe what I just said. Before I walked into class she said "Look, I've noticed he's been way too physical lately, and I've notice a change in you, please walk away from this." Nodding my head, unsure of what to say, I walked into class.

As I started to replay all of the overly touchy moments, I recognized a behavior of physical and emotional abuse. I didn't know it when it was happening but I knew it then and I knew it would be hard to get away. I told him in person "it's over, I can't do this anymore" he replied, "you don't mean that" and he walked away.

The next day he followed me to every class and blew up my phone. My nerves were shot and I was shaking. I couldn't concentrate and every time the bell had rung, I was scared to go out in the hallway. It became hard to sleep. I would toss and turn for nights without end. This went on for a few weeks and I finally gained the courage to walk up to him and say "I'm serious, I've lost all respect for you and I don't want anything to do with you." The texts became less frequent and slowly but surely he was out of my life.

There's just some people you can't change but with my heart and my perspective on life, I thought I could change the world, one person at a time. Maybe I couldn't with him but there's many others out there who still need saving. As I went on through my school year I noticed I wasn't the same person. That change the world perspective was lost and I started to trust less and less people.

There was a change in my heart, my mind, and my soul. Every day I lost a part of myself. With every word and hit, he slowly took away my confidence, my happiness, and my trust and I didn't even realize it. I never really told anyone about it. I didn't want anyone to know how badly I was breaking inside.

As the days got longer, I started to feel lost. I felt like I had no one to go to. In every direction, I saw a heartbreak waiting to happen. I didn't know who to turn to. Was this because of Him or the tragic occurrences? How did I get here? Where exactly is here?

Strength is key. Strength was the one thing I struggled with, the one thing I was looking for that wasn't easy to find. Wasn't I already strong? I'm still here aren't I?

When you go through an abusive relationship, it tears you up inside. It makes you feel worthless, unwanted, unloved. Your nerves are constantly triggered and you replay every second of it in your head, like a broken record player, It went on and on. Keep in mind I was 14 at the time. I didn't know how to handle this. At this time I did believe in God but I didn't really have a relationship with him, which may be the very reason I questioned my strength. I wasn't getting the answers I wanted so I looked for someone to blame. My dad was the target, which led to a greater gap in our relationship. I questioned a lot about his character. I would soon figure out that there's so much more to the story. Until I knew the truth almost every time I went to his house, we would fight, verbally.

For years I wanted to be close with him but as I found out more and more about his past, I began to rethink. At this time I was so broken already. So the constant battle with him wasn't always his fault. I just needed someone to blame for all my issues. Don't get me wrong, we did have our reasons to fight but most of the time he contributed more than I did. One thing that always got to me was when he made fun of my faws. I saw my flaws but I didn't think anyone else could see them. This also contributed to the lessening of my confidence. Little did he know, his little girl was losing hope. This "great sadness" continued throughout the year and got stronger every day. Ms. Frans, my science teacher, noticed and often tried to cheer me up. She would put little notes on my desk that said "I think you are awesome" and "to make you smile today." I knew once I stepped on her classroom, for forty minutes, I would be safe. I was so happy that someone cared enough to try to change my mood. She wouldn't be the only one.

She didn't know what I was going through and the fact that she took time out of she day to let me know she cared, meant more to me then she would ever know. It's those little acts of kindness that can save a life.

Later in the year I saw Coach at school hockey games. Knowing about my "great sadness" she hugged me, nudged me and always tried to lighten my mood and as I've said before, she's not usually one to show her feelings. She usually had a smart remark almost every time I talked to her. She was another one that had kept me going.

Our relationship was growing stronger by the day. I wish I could've known that when I stepped on her ice, It wouldn't ever be just about hockey, because to me she wasn't just a coach. From this point in my life, to the next milestone, and future achievements, she would be there. The year continued on and I began to find my way back to some type of normalcy. As I started to get back into my former self, summer was on it's way. I felt so relieved to be done with the school year. Walking out the front doors of Lampade High School, I looked back again, knowing that I wouldn't forget this year. Even though I would be back in the spring. It felt good to close the door and shut out all of the pain I encountered, as if it would be that easy to let go of it all.

Chapter 2 A Summer Like No Other

Schools out, finally. I love summer because I can lay around and do absolutely nothing. This summer however, was different. I was after some answers. I wanted to find out more about my family, my background, and in some ways I wanted to figure out what just happened this past year. I definitely needed a break from all the stress school brings. For some teens my age their summer bucket lists consists of creative ideas that for some reason, would sounds crazy at any other time of the year. My bucket list went a little something like this; meet your sister, spend time with your family, and more importantly revive yourself. I needed to get back on track. I needed to trace my routes.

A few weeks in and I've mostly just been at my dads, spending time with my step mom and brothers. My baby brothers give me overwhelming happiness. There's something unique about the relationship with a baby or even a toddler. Kids have a very special way of showing affection. They love you unconditionally and remind you that the tradition of family is still very much alive. Their hearts are made out of gold, their intentions are pure, and they are easily amused.

The best part of me is being their big sister, I think that will always be my greatest joy in life. When you have someone looking up to you, it makes you feel stronger. I'm a big sister and that's a huge honor and privilege. This is something I lost sight of at various moments. I sometimes forget that I have little ones watching my every move. I hug my brothers tight every time I leave my dad's house just because it's like hugging a ball of joy.

Time was running out. Although I would've loved to be with my brothers all summer, I had much to do. A couple week after I left my dad's house, I received a call from my Aunt who had just moved back to buffalo for the summer. She was asking me if I would babysit her little girl at the fair, so she could work. Of course I took the opportunity. Keep in mind, we were very close at this time. I couldn't wait for her to come home. So the fact that I would get to spend time with her and my little cousin was great news for me.

Every year my dad and stepmom bring all of us to the fair. They get to eat delicious food while we get to go on rides, it was a win win. I had my bags packed and all ready to go. My dad, my stepmom, and my little brothers, along with my cousins, were on our way to go to the fair, where I would see my aunt for the first time in two years. Family is huge for me so whenever I get to see a family member, I always get excited. On the way there I couldn't help but have a goofy smile on my face. I could barely sit still.

We had arrived and I was jumping with excitement. My cousins and I were just about to go on a ride and my brother sat out because it didn't interest him. He never really liked rides that went upside down. I was on the ride and was just about finished settling down in my seat, when I spotted her. My aunt walks up with her hair pulled back, dressed in a striped shirt with jeans and pushing my little cousin in a little toy car.

She greeted my brother with a hug and sat on the bench parked in front of the ride I was on. My brother is always awkward in these situations so he just sat down with her and didn't speak a word. Just my luck, she comes before the ride starts. I was squirming in my seat like how a dog's tail wags before he/she gets a treat.

Throughout the ride, I thought about how I was going to give her a huge hug without suffocating her. I'm a very affectionate person, always have been, always will be. The ride came to a stop and I flew out of my seat. I was running to her and it felt like a movie scene until she ran the opposite way. That's my aunt for you, always has to ruin the moment. She was joking and eventually I got my hug. I don't know what it was about this moment but I felt so relieved. It felt good to hug the person that you've wanted to see for the longest time. The next few days, I knew would be the best days of this year.

Three days. That's the time I had, to make up for years of lost time. On the way back to the hotel, my aunt's husband was asking me what I like from tim horton's for breakfast. I said "a bagel." He replied "do you like coffee?" I replied "Yes, medium double double." My aunt interrupted and said "see she's just like me." A smile on my face followed.

We arrived at the hotel and the motel. My aunt's husband dropped us off and went to stay with his friend which means I had my aunt all to myself. We chatted for hours. It was like we've been together all this time. You know when a close friend moves away and then comes back to visit and things are just like it use to be. That how it felt only, we weren't really close until months prior to this. Although we had to get up at 7a.m, we talked till 3a.m. We mostly talked about family and told old stories that resulted in both of us laughing till the crack of dawn.

Eventually I had to ask. I just had to ask if she knew about my long lost sister. With a little hesitation, she replied "yes, I saw her not too long ago at Tiny's." Tiny is also my aunt, at this time I didn't know much about her. My aunt when on and on about how my sister wanted to meet me too. I finally would check mark on my bucket list. My aunt gave me her number and now I to get know my sister. This added onto the rebuilding of my heart.

This was my opportunity to find the answers to all the questions I had asked previously. It was weird though I didn't really know how to start the conversation. What do I even say? "Hi, this is your sister that you've never met before. What's up?" Yeah right. I thought about it for a couple hours and I finally texted her. I vaguely remember saying "Hello, this is Nevaeh. Auntie gave me your number." As soon as I sent it, my aunt texted me telling me where to meet her for lunch.

I quickly rushed to meet her. I greeted her with a hug, as always, even though I just saw her a few moments ago. My aunt isn't a very mushy person. She's not good with showing affection which is completely opposite from me. If I love you, I will let you know, no problem. After lunch we headed our separate ways and me and her baby went to the park by the fair. I love watching kids run around.

What I wouldn't give to be that age again and to not have a worry in the world. The park is where me and the baby went for most of the day. We made up little games to play to occupy our time. The games you play with kids never make sense but you play them anyways because you love how happy it makes them. After about six hours, It was time to go back to the motel. As the fair was closing for the night, I took one good look and the Ferris wheel. It lit up in different colors and stood tall. It kept going round and round, just like life, it goes on.

It was the last night and I was trying to enjoy it as much as I could. When my Aunt is tired, A switch in her head turns on and all the sudden she's the funniest person on the planet. That whole night, she had me laughing hysterically. Her baby was out like a light and here we are crying, from laughing so hard. I think we were so tired, we just laughed at everything and anything. It doesn't make sense now but it made sense at the time. It was like 2 a.m and we couldn't keep our eyes open anymore. Off to bed.

I woke up the next morning and realized it was the last day with my aunt and her baby. Since I was babysitting at the fair, I had my friends come and hangout with me for this last day. They saw me and said, "Nevaeh, you look so happy." I had a moment of realization. This whole time, I didn't think once about all the things that hurt me this year which is good right? Did I move forward right way or did I just ignore it? I can't believe how much this weekend lifted my spirit. My friends and I walked around the fair for what felt like an hour and already the fair was closing. I hugged each one goodbye and met up with my aunt.

It was time. Time to say goodbye to my aunt and her baby. I had a very short ride home in which I looked at my aunts baby with a smile. I had an awesome time with her and my love for her and kids in general, grew. The car came to a stop which meant I was home. I must've given my aunt five hugs. It was so hard for me to let go. In some ways, I knew that saying goodbye would take a piece of my heart. I didn't realize it but I was so vulnerable and still a little broken. That's what I really like about my aunt, her ability to make all around her incredibly happy. She distracted me without even knowing she was doing it.

I hugged her one last time and went over to the driver side where her husband was sitting. I looked at him and said "promise me something, That you'll bring her back to me." He replied with a smile "Of course." My aunt looked at me in an awe look and said "Don't worry, I'll see you again soon." As she pulled out of my driveway, I looked back again. Another moment, I felt a knot in my stomach. How do I miss her already? One major thing I learned from this week, I was going to be okay. I can scratch off, revive yourself.

It was back to the drawing board. I technically haven't met my sister but our conversations became more frequent. What I didn't take into consideration is how my dad would feel, how everybody would feel about my decision to talk to her. I was always thinking of others but for right now I needed to think of myself. She's suppose to be family. For me, family has always been a priority so you could imagine my disappointment when I had to meet my sister at 15. For reasons that will remain unsaid, the meeting of my sister and I was very discouraged. Despiste how many people would be mad, we arranged to meet the day before school at my sisters boxing class.

My dad found out at and called me. He said, very strictly, "What do you think you're doing?" I replied "getting to know my sister" as my stomach twisted and I started shaking he said, "I don't want you talking to her, delete her number." Holding back the tears, I said "okay" and hung up. I was with my best friend Khloe at the time and we were shopping at target. I immediately bursted into tears and again, my nerves were shot.

When we got back to khloe's house her mom hugged me. Her mom was like my mom and I told her everything. Crying hysterically, I tried to tell her what happened. When I was done telling her, she looked at me with a worried look. She didn't know what to say, I mean what the hell do you say at this point. She said "calm down, I'm sure everything will work itself out." I took a deep breathe and I calmed down.

The phone rung and it was my step mom. She called not to yell at me, but to better understand the situation. I again had to tell the story. After I said my last word, she said "Nevaeh, It's a very complicated situation. I understand both sides of this but you need to understand that there's much more to the story. If you want to meet your sister, no one can stop you." We hung up the phone and I took a deep breath. I could finally breathe. This phone call left me with much to think about. I didn't want to hurt my dad but I had to meet her.

Going against my dad, I texted her and we arranged the time and day to meet. I did feel a little guilty, I knew a lot of people discouraged our meeting for a reason. I was scared of what it would do to me and my dad's relationship but you don't chose your family, It's just arranged for you. So technically, she is family and me being the way I am, I didn't want her to feel alone, I wanted her to know she has a family here for her. We worked out all the details and with the support from my mom and my aunt, I was able to feel a little more at ease and follow through on our arrangements.

The day came sooner then expected. We were on our way, As my mom and I got closer and closer to the boxing class, my nerves bursted under my skin like a rocket launched off to the moon. Car rides with my mom are unique. She turns on a good song and make me laugh by dancing to it. I think she was trying to comfort me. That is what's so great about my mom, she always knows how to make me laugh.

We finally arrived and as I got out of the car my legs started to shake and with each step it felt like my knees were giving out. My mom tried to calm me down and soon enough I laughed it off, as I said to myself, "What? Did you forget to walk you moron?" I regained confidence as my mom opened the entrance. There she was. My sister. She stood tall like a christmas tree, she was built and had this conservative way about her. As the class went on we followed the instructor's directions while we conversated about ourselves. We discussed our likes and dislikes, our past, present and future, Our wildest dreams and biggest wishes. After a very short hour the class ended and my mom took a picture of us to capture the moment, as if we would ever forget.

I owe her the biggest thank you for bringing me to my sister.It meant the world to me, having that time with my sister. I enjoyed every part of it and from that point on we talked more and more. As we were building up some kind of relationship, we arranged more dates to hangout. What a great way to end a beautiful summer. I checked off everything on my bucket list or so I thought.

Chapter 3 ROUND 2

Well, it was the first day of school. As the first bell rung, every student tried to regain some type of attention. My first class was English. I always liked English, something about poets and writers from a different time caught my attention and throughout my highschool years, my interests in this specific subject grew. One of our firsts assignments that we had to complete was writing a letter to ourselves about our hopes, dreams, and a very quick summary of our summer. At this time, all I could think about was how eventful my summer had been.

I was all in my head and started to flashback to the memories of the months prior. I was caught in a memory when the bell rung to symbolize the end of the period. I looked down at my blank paper and thought "way to make a good first impression, you had one job." I laughed as I moved to my next class. The day went on like any other until I got to my last class Mrs. Milanos class which happened to also be science.

This teacher would one day be the very reason I made it through the year ahead. The first quarter went by surprisingly fast. I was pretty confident in myself that I wouldn't let this year turn out like freshman year. This was going to be my year, The year my grades were above average, my memories were filled with nothing but laughter, my intentions pure, and my heart full of gold. Only, the year from here on out would be everything but ordinary.

Sometime before Christmas everyone I spoke with seemed to have been the "bearer of bad news." The first unsettling event was my sister ignoring all my texts and calls. Things were going so well and I thought that we were on the verge of building a strong relationship. Every text, call, and voicemail was disregarded by her. I didn't get an explanation and that was the worst part. I felt so disappointed and frustrated. I kept wondering why she left. She was just getting to know me, how did she already want an out? I went over every memory in my head and found nothing. I couldn't answer my own questions and I knew I wouldn't get them from her.

I turned to our aunt Tiny. She's a very special person to my sister. As close as I was to my aunt, she was just as close to Tiny. I texted her with tears streaming down my face "Do you know why my sister isn't speaking to me?" she replied, "No, I haven't heard anything. Maybe she's just busy." I cried harder, hitting another dead end. I didn't know who else to ask or talk to, so I tried to shake it off and focus even harder on school.

Assignments were piling up and more bad news was coming. My mom sat me down and said, with a worried look on her face "Nevaeh, your Uncle Joey is very sick. The doctors say he has about a year to live." I didn't really know my uncle Joey but it was like an alarm set off in my head, here comes the waterworks. I called him shortly after and left a voicemail, "Hey Uncle joey it's Nevaeh, Shayla's daughter, I wanted to let you know I'm thinking of you, If you could give me a call back, I would love to chat with you." About a week later he called back. After an hour of talking we found a lot of common interests. I just realized I have this down to earth Uncle and haven't spent anytime with him. Again I tried to blame myself.

We started to text almost everyday and got closer with each word. I started to feel a little relief as we arranged to see a movie on a thursday night after hockey practice. We had to wait until it was a little warm considering it was winter time and he was very sick. Luckily we live in Buffalo where the weather is all over the place, and on that thursday night it hit fifty degrees.

On our ride down to the movie we kept talking about God and our faith. That was all we talked about leading up to the movie. Throughout the whole conversation, the thing that stood out most was when he was telling me how he got cancer.

He said, "I was in the hospital for pneumonia and I saw all of these sick kids, it broke my heart. Later that night when I got home I prayed and prayed to God and asked him to take away the sickness from those kids and give it to me. A few months later I found out I had cancer. Wanna know something?" I struggled to not let a single tear out and replied, "what?" he replied, "I wouldn't change anything that happened to me. If I could just save one kids life, I'm more than happy to do it." I was in shock with amazement. I couldn't believe what I just heard. I smiled, turned to the window and said in my head "My Uncle is amazing."

We arrived at the movie theatre which was inside a mall. As we were walking from the car to the theater, He kept pausing, and told me "I really have to sit down." I looked at him with a worried look and replied "okay, let's sit." I knew he was weak and that he was putting on a brave face for me.

We continued on our walk there, paid for our tickets and made it to our seats, where we conversated more and more about God and life.

He said "I have this friend who I often debate with about whether God is real or not. I turned to my friend and said okay let's say he's not real and I spend all my life following the commandments and preaching the bible, when I die nothings going to happen. But let's say he is real, then I've spent my whole life praying and believing and I go straight up to Heaven and you've spent all of your life believing in science." He continued with the greatest look on his face, "He had nothing left to say."

I looked at him with a great big smile as the commercials came to an end and the movie began. Popcorn in hand, eyes on screen, and 3D glasses on. I enjoyed every second of it. After a short 2 hours the movie ended and we headed back to my house. You'll never guess what we talked about on the way home. God and life. The best conversations I ever had was with him and God.

We arrived at my house and I invited him in. My dog Dunkin, yes like the coffee shop, ran towards us and greeted him with a giant leap into his arms. My sister and brother came down the stairs and my mom was waiting in the kitchen. We all sat in a circle on the kitchen floor, which is unusual but I don't think anyone cared. We conversated for a while and during this time he had a sparkle in his eye. With every word he spoke he had a big, goofy grin to follow. I love his smile.

Well back to school the next day. I texted my uncle everyday and we were very close. It's crazy to think how fast we bonded. The next couple weeks were peaceful. It felt like the calm before a storm. I felt a knot in my stomach but no need to worry because Christmas was now here. Presents are wrapped and the lights on the tree are glistening brighter than ever. Around the holidays I'm usually very happy but this year I wasn't. I couldn't shake this feeling and I'm still unsure of what that feeling was.

I was now on Christmas break and I spent most of my nights, shivering between the covers and crying in my pillow. I was sad and as much as I've tried to ignore it, it broke through the brick wall I put up. I found myself waiting for something else to happen. Waiting for the storm to pass. What I didn't know is that the Storm hasn't even started. I received more bad news.

I was upstairs in the bathroom late at night and I was crying quietly. I definitely didn't want my mom or grandparents hearing me. I looked in the mirror and saw tears streaming down my face, I got on my knees, put my hands together and started praying to God, "Please God, take the pain away. I can't do this on my own." When you're looking at yourself in the mirror and you're no longer happy with yourself and your life, it destroys your soul.

As I finished my prayer, I dried my eyes and went downstairs to look for ibuprofen since all of my crying gave me a headache. I saw my grandma standing in the kitchen which I thought was odd since it was late. She looked at me and told me that my cousin overdosed on heroin and that he is at the hospital with my uncle. I was so frustrated that I kept receiving bad news. I grunted and went back upstairs to lay down. I didn't even ask how he was doing because I was so wrapped up in what was going on in my life. My heart is now broken at this point.

For the past few weeks it had been nothing but bad news. I was frustrated with the constant heart breaking words of "Nevaeh, there's something I need to tell you" or "Did you hear about so and so?" I just couldn't take anymore. I was so in my head for weeks that I noticed my grades started to drop a little but I had time to fix it. Besides I'm on Christmas break.

I absolutely love the holidays as most people do. Any time I get to see my family it brightens my mood. This year however, it was different because I got to spend it with my uncle Joey. I spend Christmas morning with my grandparents, my mom and a couple of my siblings. I spend the rest with my dad and stepmom. This year we made a pit stop at my other grandparents house. I saw my uncle and immediately ran to give him a hug. We took a picture to capture our first Christmas together.

That was such a special moment for me. I could tell though, that he wasn't feel particularly well but he of course had a big ole' grin on his face. Which assured me he was okay. When we left that day, I didn't know that would be the last time I would ever get to hug him.

We arrived at my dads. The best thing about my family is that my mom and dad, although separated, have been able to stay friends so it makes it easier on everyone. My mom and stepmom are best friends. I know, unusual but we like it that way. Every year, I get my step mom a gift that I think will bring her to tears and this year I definitely did. I put a picture of us in a frame and captioned it "I'm lucky because I get to have my best friend as my step mom." It's the giving part of the holidays that makes me love it.

The holidays brightened me up for a little while. Until I heard my Uncle don had mini strokes and was by himself for days until he got to the phone to call for help. He was now in the hospital, unable to talk and he could barely move. It broke whatever was left of my heart. My family was falling apart piece by piece, person by person.

New years was right around the corner and I always spend it with my little brothers. As we drove to my dad's house my mom said "So Nevaeh, I'm not really suppose to know this but I overheard that Jack isn't doing good." Jack is a family-friend but really he's like another grandpa to me. I just looked at her and said "really?" because honestly I didn't know what to say. I'm in the middle of fighting an inner battle and it was starting to get harder and harder to keep it from my family.

I feel so deeply for people. When I heard that Jack wasn't doing well, I wasn't thinking about how it would affect me. I was thinking about how it would affect my grandparents and his wife. I wouldn't be able to see them like that.

I turned to my aunt who I knew could help me out. I texted her days after new years, she was my go to person. She knew everything that was happening and she is really good with helping me cope. I always admired her for the way she took on problems a step at a time and how she can help me identify things about myself that I wouldn't see otherwise.

For the past year she had been the person who pushed ms every step of the way. She didn't let me give up. When I say my aunt is my favorite person, it's because she knows everything about me and has stuck with me through every storm. Just like the storm I was about to face.

Chapter 4 My Breaking Point

The storm had arrived. The first week I lost the battle. It was hard for me to do simple tasks like getting out of bed in the morning. I immediately turned to my go to person. My aunt quickly responded and said the most encouraging words. At this time she was back home, across the world. I didn't get to see her before she left but we still kept in touch everyday.

I think she was trying to avoid this downfall. She wanted me to identify that I was not okay but I couldn't face it. For days I tried to convince her that I was fine but at that point I was just lying to myself. This life it's a spiritual battle, you're constantly trying to figure out how life works, and what's the next step.

During this time I didn't think I was going to see the sun shine the next day. I was so broken. Completely broken. Everyday I got up was just another day that I wanted to end. The best way I can explain this is that it's like you feel everything at once but at the same time, you feel nothing at all. I was putting up a fight with this part of me for so long that I was emotionally tired. I was exhausted from pretending I was okay. I wasn't okay and I haven't been since freshman year.

One of the days in school when I was carrying this with me, I had a traumatic experience. I had my headphones plugged in and I tuned out everyone. I started to feel like I was floating in mid air. I looked down and saw myself sitting there looking off in the distance, almost as if I was empty. For what felt like hours, I was watching myself from above. The bell rung and I was startled. My nerves were flared up and I was so scared not knowing what just happened. I was in shock and my first thought was to text my aunt. She replied with unbelievable words, "I think you could be schizophrenic." Reading that, I was almost positive that I wasn't.

I reassured myself that I wasn't going crazy. That same day my hockey team was going to watch an all star, women's professional game. Coach would be there and seeing her always cheers me up. That day it was different. It's like I was scared to look her in the eyes because she might be the one who see's that I'm not okay. I was nervous because she knows me almost too well.

When we arrived at the rink, I didn't see her, I felt so relieved. The first period started and I looked at the ice, glistening with all of its lines and glory. Again I tuned everyone out but this time I didn't need the headphones. Like I said, hockey is my happy place, no matter what rink. It's the atmosphere that it's created for me, that brings me joy.

My friend and teammate shook me and said we're going to take pictures. I got up and said I'll take them. We were gone less than ten minutes. When we came back, guess who was sitting in the row behind where I was previously sitting.

Coach was sitting there, laughing up a storm with my school hockey coach. I walked down to my row and walked past her like I didn't see her. She kicked me in a playful manner and a big smile and a loud hi followed. Did I mention she's very loud? That's just the kind of person she is. I replied "hey" which was very unusual for me because I usually bear hug her. She knew something was up and she of course said something. "What, are you mad at me or something?" To cover up my sadness I replied "yeah, because you never answer my texts!" Which most of the time she really didn't. To be fair, when it was important she was the quickest responder. I turned back around after some laughs shared. I felt relieved again because she didn't notice.

Moments later, My aunt texted me encouraging me to tell someone. At this time since she was overseas she could only help to a certain extent. I said "Nobody listens" and she replied "what about your mom or samantha (my sister), or your stepmom?" I thought about it and replied "My mom always thinks I'm overreacting and me and my sister aren't that close, she would probably laugh at me. I don't want to worry my step mom." Quickly she responded "Please try Nevaeh, this is serious, I think they will listen." I continued to watch the game and thought about how the conversation might go.

The game ended shortly after. I couldn't believe it. I barely watched it, was my love for hockey fading away? The bus ride home I was all in my head again. I sat down next to my best friend at the time and started to open up to her. She said the same thing "I think you should tell someone." When I got home I ran upstairs. My sister said something mean in a joking manner, as always. I said in a very serious voice "I'm seriously not in the mood." She came in my room and asked what was wrong. I said "Nothing" which is the natural response. You just say nothing because you don't think that they care enough. She said "No Nevaeh, seriously what's wrong." I started bawling my eyes out. "Samantha I'm so scared of myself. I'm so sad and I don't know what to do anymore."

I've never really had a serious conversation with my sister, we just weren't close in that way. She looked at me with a look I've never seen before, almost as if she was worried. My mom walked in nervously and was wondering what all the commotion was about. As I cried harder in front of my family, I tried to explain to the best of my ability that I didn't know what was going on but I do know that I don't like the way I feel. I went to my bed where my family was sitting and took a deep breathe before the waterworks came again. My sister sat there speechless. I don't think anyone really knew what to say. They were so in shock that I felt this way. I was always a happy go lucky type of kid. Growing up around a sarcastic family, that just the way I was. For them to see me like this was probably hard but for me to let them see me like this was even harder.

I come from a strong family, everyone is strong in their own way. My strength disappeared in the midst of all the heartbreak. My grandma eventually entered in and was filled in. The night was unusual. No one really knew what to do, what to say, or how to feel. We all sat there in silence for a few moments as they comoforted me. The one thing I kept thinking about was how I got this deep and how I was going to get out.

School the next day was a blur. I kept to myself with my headphones in and music blasting. I didn't pay attention in any of my classes, not even my favorite class, science. Mrs. Milano noticed and said something like "Is everything okay?" I replied honestly this time because for some reason I felt like I could really trust her. I began to explain that I was overwhelmed and didn't feel like myself. She looked at me and didn't really know what to say either. Honestly, what do you say? How do you help someone who's barely holding on? She comforted me to the best of her ability.

After some very encouraging words I headed home. I went upstairs and just lost it. Tears came bursting out. My head fell to pillow and my body curled up. I felt a sudden cold rush through my body. I kept thinking over and over what's happening? My aunt texted to check up on me and I told her about my day. She was always a funny person, every joke had me laughing so hard I could barely breathe. She made a joke at the end of our conversation that read "don't go floating anywhere." I chuckled a little, then had a flashback to that moment in school. I was now shaking in fear and ever more scared then I was before. I then remembered that I hadn't eaten anything all day.

If you know my family, you know that we all eat a lot. More than the common folk. So to hear that one of us went a whole day without eating is unheard of. At that point I didn't care and couldn't bring myself to eat anything anyways. My stomach felt so different for weeks. It was like when you go on a date for with someone you really like and you get what's known as "butterflies", that's how it felt but it wasn't for the same reason. This uncomfortable knot in my stomach is from anxiety. My mom suffers from anxiety and I've seen how it affect her. Now I feel what she's felt for years. I couldn't shake this feeling, I couldn't wish it away. I was stuck with it.

The next day was even harder. I mentally and emotionally didn't have the strength to get out of bed. I couldn't put on makeup and dress for another day. Let alone for a school day. My mom growing more worried, let me stay home. I didn't sleep much the last few days and even if I went, I wouldn't really be there. My mind would be elsewhere. That's what sucks, with depression you miss everything.

Every part of your day is drained by overwhelming pain. All I wanted to do is cry and that's all I did. I sat in my room all day and again didn't eat much. The hardest part of the day was looking my mom in the eyes. I'm not a parent but I know it's hard to see your kid suffering. It was really hard on my mom. Almost every time she looked at me, she struggled to hold back the tears.

My mom is a great mom. My depression was not her fault in any way, shape, or form. I think for a while she thought it was. I could hear her talking downstairs to my grandparents and I could tell by the tone of her voice, she was heartbroken. That's what I wanted to avoid. I didn't want my family to blame themselves for my sadness. That's the reason I kept it from them for so long but since I kept it all in, it was just a bomb waiting to explode. The day went by so slow. The tears kept coming and half of the day I sat in silence, or at least I tried to.

I heard voice in my head. They mumbled their words and I was too scared to try to figure out what they were saying. After a while, I couldn't take it anymore so I turned on the t.v and tried to drown them out as much as I could. Slowly but surely I didn't hear them. I slept for a good half hour before I woke up shaking. I had an anxiety dream, I felt like I was falling down an endless hole. I was startled and then realized I woke up to the same sadness I tried to sleep off. The waterworks were back.

School wasn't even a question the next day. I looked even worse. My mom called the doctor and scheduled an appointment. My grandpa always takes me to my appointments and I didn't want him to see my like this either. My grandpa and I have always been close. He's always been there for me and we have a very strong relationship. He always cheers me up but at this time nothing was helping. My mom ended up taking me. On the way to the doctor's office, I plugged in my music and leaned my head against the window.

When we arrived I was more than anxious. We were immediately called back. In the room there was a small, rectangular window that overlooked the sky and a big tree. I sat looking out the window thinking of absolutely nothing. The doctor walked in and asked me the questions. "Do you sleep? Do you have thoughts of committing suicide? Has your appetite changed?" My sarcastic self popped into my mind quickly. If I was myself I would say "No, I'm just here for fun" but I wasn't myself. Which made me cry. What happened to me? My mom answered the questions for me. The doctor officially stated I was depressed and gave me a prescription for medicine.

To hear that I was officially at a low point, killed me. I always thought I was strong enough to make it through anything, little did I know that I was hitting rock bottom. So this is what it's like? I always wondered why they called it "rock bottom". Maybe its because you're officially at the bottom. Maybe life is like climbing a rock wall. Sometimes you make it all the way up to the top and other times you can't hold yourself up and you fall to the ground. That's how I looked at it.

The next day my mom brought up the idea of talking to a priest. At this time I didn't have the best relationship with God. I didn't want to leave the house let alone talk to anyone. I knew if I agreed, it would make her feel better, so I did. She called and there was no answer. I spent the day laying in bed, crying. The usual, typical day for me lately.

During this week I kept getting asked the same two questions. "What's wrong?" and more frequently asked by my mom and grandma "Did something else happen?" Which triggered more emotions. Was all the was happening not enough to drive me to this sadness? And what's wrong? So many things. They knew the answers to their own question, I just think they didn't know what else to say.

One day my mom came in my room and sat on the bed. She was doing her usual check in. She gave me a hug and again I started crying. She whispered "It's okay baby girl, It's going to be okay." I let go and laid back down as she left the room and closed the door behind her. When she left I looked up at my ceiling, thinking about absolutely nothing, which was nice and calming.

My phone beeped, my aunt texted. "How are you?" "I'm okay, I stayed home from school." My aunt wasn't happy that I stayed home. She didn't want me to give up, she didn't want me to lose sight of my future. At that point I already did. I lost every dream, every perspective, every aspect of life. I lost myself.

I couldn't breathe and I was so emotionally distraught. My grandma's birthday dinner was hard but I couldn't miss it. I sat at dinner, mentally lost but emotionally held together. I didn't talk much and couldn't eat much. My sister finished at the same time as I did and offered to have me ride with her. During the car ride home she said the most pivotal words of my depression. "Don't let it define you." which got me thinking.

I got home and it was back to the same old thing. My face was burried in my pillow and I let it all out. This is so hard. It's so hard to keep it all together even if it's just for an hour. I turned on the t.v and prepared myself for another sleepless night. Days just kept passing by.

One night when I was watching t.v my brother popped his head in to see if I wanted to get food. My brother and I had a unique relationship. We fought like normal siblings but we were there for each other at any given time. I thanked him for his order but knew I wasn't ready to leave the house again. He ran downstairs for ten minutes. He came in my room again and came over next to the bed and said "Look you were there for me, and now i'm gonna be there for you. Okay? I'm here, I'm here." I started to cry on his shoulder but this was more of a reliving cry. It felt nice to have that support from my brother.

My dad texted me asking me to come spend the night. He said "Hope you're feeling a little better. We can have a one on one later. I've had a hard time when I was younger too. Similar thoughts about life. And the past 2 weeks have been extremely difficult for me. So I know how you're feeling. As I get older I'm seeing more and more loved ones pass. It's difficult. So maybe I need to talk to someone as much as you do. Hopefully we can help each other." This was by far the best thing my dad could've said at that time. My dad and I weren't really close and I was surprised he would want to talk to me in a heart to heart way.

Before my mom brought me to my dads, she took me out to eat with her 3 close friends. Her friends are like my friends, and these specific friends are more like family in their own way. Susanna is like a step mom, she has always brought a positive energy into my life. Sauna is like an aunt, she always gives me bear hugs especially during this time. Before we left the house we sat on the couch and she hugged me tight, letting me know she's right there with me. Emily is like a cool, older sister, she always makes the best expression. A face is worth a thousand words. They all talked at dinner and I just sat staring at the brick wall behind my mom. One of my eyes had a bad twitch, I assume from nerve damage, so it hurt too look at lights.

Dinner ended and we headed to my dads. When I got there my step mom opened the door and she looked almost shocked. I don't think she knew how bad it was. My baby brothers, who bring me the most joy rushed to greet me at the door as my mom kissed me and said "I love you."

I went straight to the couch and watched t.v. My brother who was 4 at the time, came to me and said "why are you so sad?" Struggling to not shred a tear, I replied "I just am buddy." He squeezed me and said "I love you." My step mom who I am extremely close with and love deeply, sat besides me asking me question which I just nodded to. She got up and made me a cup of tea, she knows me too well. I love tea.

A few sips in, my dad walked in and said "let's go kick it in the basement." I got up and followed him, curious to what he was going to say. He started describing what it was like when his mom passed. He said he pushed away everyone he cared about. He then further explained

I know how you feel. My dad has been going to the hospital for the past few weeks to see my uncle Don and help him in any way that he can. He told me he was stressed and worried. I looked at my dad so differently in that moment. I never took into consideration the tragic loss my dad encountered at a young age. He went on and said "I'm sorry for not being involved in your life as much as I should be, It kills me to see you like this. What's going on?"

I explained as much as I could without crying. When I finished with everything he gave me a big hug, symbolizing the beginning of a new and improved relationship. Our relationship dramatically changed from that point on. I went back upstairs and talked to my step mom in her bedroom.

I lost it. I started crying as I said "i'm so sad and I don't know why, I can't take it anymore. I just feel like everything around me is going wrong and I just.." I could bring myself to finish my sentence. She said "nobody expects you to do this on your own. It's a lot to take in, you're only 15." she wiped the tears off my face and gave me a big hug. That's why I love my step mom. She treats me as if I'm her own. We finished talking and just looked up at the ceiling.

My step mom popped in a movie and for once I fell asleep. Only for a few hours but that's more than I've had in weeks. I woke up with brighter perspective. My baby brothers came in hugging and jumping on me. It's like they knew I needed it. They gave me so much extra love that day.

My aunt texted early that morning, "hey, are you at your dads?" I replied "yes, I spent the night" she replied "Did it help?" and surprisingly I responded "it sure did." I have the most amazing little brothers. Their ability to take their heart right out of their chest and give it to me, amazes me. They picked up a piece of my heart and glued it back to the whole, like they were finishing a puzzle.

It was time for me to leave as my mom pulled into the driveway. I definitely felt better but there was still that heart aching pain in my heart. The only thing that kept me going was the support I received from my family and friends. I received so much support. The more people that heard, the more texts I received. My phone was blowing up. Then I had a moment of realization. A lot of people care about me. I have a huge support system.

Messages from my aunt were so encouraging. Words after word she was building up my strength and pushing me to stand back up again. She was there from the very beginning and stuck by my side. I absolutely adored my aunt. She was my best friend and I trusted her with everything. I love my aunt and anybody who knows me, knows how close we are. I let them know.

At school my first stop was Mrs. Millanos room. She was so happy to see me but I was even happier to see her. She cares enough to speak up in the beginning of the hardest week of my life and it made me look at her differently. She gave a hug and told me it was good to see me.

I went to first period, I was still quiet and not like myself when my best friend came to give me a hug. She said "I'm happy your back, what's wrong with your eye?" I explained, "It's nerve damage I think, from crying and not sleeping." We continued to do our work. The day went on like any other until I arrived to art. I was taking a ceramics course with one of the bests, Mrs. Perry Smith was the greatest ceramicist I've ever met. Her passion for art is inspiring. We were in the middle of doing a project and I have always had an interest in art. There's something about the way your brain interacts with your hands to make a picture that always captured my attention. Art gives me almost the same feeling hockey gives me. When I'm channeling my energy into my artwork I lose myself in a good way. One of my mom's friends Roy, who is a very passionate Christian and a very loving human being, texted me. He assured me I'm not alone and that he's praying for me. His text made my day. I adore him.

The year went on because as my aunt once told me "you have to keep going because life doesn't stop for anybody. You may wanna take a break but life goes on with or without you." She's always been hard on me in a good way. Sometimes even too hard. Summer was already around the corner and I was happy to have a break from school and a time to heal but until then I had to focus and get back to being the good student I use to be.

My school hockey team had a game today and they were facing Coach's team. I had to go, so I hopped on the bus with my eye still twitching, hoping that my love for the game would heal some wounds. I couldn't play with my eye the way it was but I loved watching too. When we arrived I walked into the rink and took a deep breathe. I love the smell of the ice, especially on game day. I sat down and looked at the scoreboard as i pictured what the score will be. Then I heard her.

Coach is extremely loud as I've previously stated. Her voice traveled closer and closer until she stood right next me. "Why aren't you playing?" I knew that as soon as I looked at her she would see I was hurting. I looked at her and pointed to my eye "I can't really ee much out of my eye, and I haven't been to practice in a while." She replied, "I see that. What happened?" "It's nerve damage." Time stood still. She was waiting for me to finish and I was trying to build up courage to tell her. She's like a role model to me, I didn't want her to see me this way. I finally got some words out as I said "It's from crying and not sleeping." She looked at me and responded "I get it, I've been in the same position lately." I was so caught up in my own world I didn't even notice she wasn't doing so well. She went on to explain that she was going through a low point as well. I looked at her shocked and speechless. She continued on and said "You know I'm here for you right?" I responded "Well I know you're busy, I don't want to bother you." She gave me one of those what the heck are you talking about looks as she said "I don't care how busy I am. I'm always here for you, you can always come to me." She leaned over and gave me a hug.

Coach has never been the type to give out hugs. I usually just hug her as she stands still. It was very unusual for her to initiate it. It amazed me how much that cheered me up. I have a very deep respect and appreciation for Coach. For her to do that was the best medicine. She walked away and went on to do the thing she does best, coach. I watched my team lose but just watching my favorite sport was very healing.

From this day on I continued to get up in the morning, everyday it got a little easier. I continued to have amazing support from my family and friends which was a big help. As a family the best thing you can do is just be there for the person that's struggling. Encourage them to make that first step at getting up in the morning but don't overstep.

I think once you get depression, it's the hardest thing to come back from. If you've never had depression, you don't understand the feeling and that's where most people are mistaken. You're constantly battling yourself and you see the world as one dark tunnel. There's always a light at the end of the tunnel, I just had to search for it.

Chapter 5 THE COMEBACK

This was the hard part. It wasn't battling depression, it was coming out of it that would be the real fight. It's not easy to do and I knew that the day It all started. I had just lost myself for so long and I lost the fight. I let depression win but now I'm asking for a rematch. I wanted a rematch, I was going to fight for myself like I had never done before.

The first step to getting over my depression was counseling. The medicine, it never really helped. It just delayed my upbringing. My aunt once said to me, "those meds, they're not going to help you. You need help, you need to talk to someone." My aunt was never one to sugar coat things. She told it how it was and didn't think twice. For a long time she had been the person I trusted everything with. She was family but more importantly she was my person. No matter what it was I needed, or what I was going through I knew I could come to her. Something changed because this summer I lost her along with a very special person in my life.

I was shopping with my mom when my aunt Tessa called. "Hey sweetie, How are you doing?" I replied, "I'm great and yourself?" In a confused tone she said, "Really? Well that's good to hear." She hung up and I questioned what that was all about. Nobody calls just to check up on me. My phone rang again. My cousin Vanessa asked the same questions and again was surprised at my answers. When she hung up I wondered why they asked the same questions. My aunt Tessa called again. "Honey, no one told you did they?" As I was walking out of the store I replied, "Told me what?" Her voice was a little shaky when she broke the news, "Uncle Joey passed away, I'm so sorry sweetie."

At first I didn't say a word. I didn't want to believe it and then it poured out of me. I was crying hysterically as my mom repeatedly asked me what happened. When I finally could slow down enough to take a deep breath and talk, I told her. Tears began to roll down her cheeks. Uncle Joey was an amazing person. That's so rare to find these days. We knew that this day was coming but I thought that we had more time. My uncle is a hero and the best kind. He was so dedicated to his faith and genuinely cared about people, no matter what they looked like, who they were, how they acted. My uncle is an inspiration to me. The way he lived was so inspiring, he was selfless.

When I got home I ran upstairs and bawled my eyes out. He was planning to come to my Confirmation in April, one of the biggest days of my life. I was upset that I wouldn't get to share that day with him or any other days for rest of my life. My first thought was to go to my aunt but she wasn't responding. I just sat in my room looking at the ceiling. Can I get a break? Just a little time to breathe. For once in my life I just wanted my life to be boring. I didn't ask for this. I didn't ask for heartbreak but it was given to me and this wasn't the last time it was coming.

As we prepared for the memorial service, which didn't happen till a month later, I asked if I could to the eulogy. Writing has always been therapeutic for me. The way I could type all the things my heart was saying but my mouth couldn't find the words, it was healing. It let me drown my sorrows. It took me a while to type it but once I did I asked my teacher to read it over. In class, we were watching a movie and she sat on the side at one of the tables. I handed her the eulogy and headed back to my seat. I glanced over a few times to see her reaction to it.

At the end of the period she handed it back to me and asked, "Did you write this all by yourself?" I replied, "yeah why?" She said, "It's very well written I liked it alot." I poured my heart on to those pages. I wanted it to speak everything my heart was screaming. I read over it millions of times, questioning whether or not it was good enough. Until I realized that as long as it came from the heart, It would be everything I wanted it to be.

The day came closer and closer and the more I read over it, the more nervous I became. When it was finally time to get ready for the funeral, My nervous calmed. I reassured myself that I would do great besides, my guardian angel will be right there with me. Before I knew it, it was time to go. We drove to meet everybody and it was just moments before I had to go up. I had my speech ready and I was ready. The priest said, "Nevaeh is now going to speak a few words."

My eulogy read as follows,

There's this quote that reads "If tears could build a stairway and memories a lane, we would walk right up to heaven, and bring you home again. No farewell words were spoken, no time to say goodbye, you were gone before we knew it and only God knows why. Our hearts still ache in sadness and secret tears still flow, what it meant to lose you, no one will ever know. But now we know you want us to mourn for you no more, To remember the happy times, life still has much in store. Since you'll never be forgotten, we pledge to you today, A hallowed place within our hearts is where you'll always stay". I must've read that quote almost a hundred times because It's something Uncle Joey would've loved. If you knew joey you knew how immensely he cared for people and for life. He was never worried about himself, he was worried about the people around him. I remember just a couple of months ago we were going to the mall to see Moby Dick which was one of his favorite movies growing up. On our way down there we started a conversation that revolved around the topic of God. He went on and on about faith and life in general. As we started to get into the depth of our talk I noticed how much he really appreciated life and family. You could see it in his eyes, He loved his family and he loved this life, his life. He then went into detail about a talk he had with God. He was describing how he was in the hospital for pneumonia and he saw all of these little kids, kids who have their whole life ahead of them, sick, very sick, cancer sick. He begged God to take it away from all of those little kids and give it to him and eventually he did. You wouldn't believe what he said next, He said he definitely doesn't regret what he asked God to do and he would never change what happened to him. After hearing those words come from my uncle's mouth I then had a moment of realization of how amazing of a person he is, He doesn't help people to make him feel better about himself he does it out of the kindness of his heart. He was such a real, down to earth person. They don't come like that anymore. His heart was bigger than earth itself. He was always giving as much as he could and wasn't looking for anything back in return. I think we all know joey was a talker. He loved to talk, it didn't matter what he said but how he said it. He said every word with passion like it would be his last. He loved everyday like it would be his last and he lived everyday like it would be his last. Thank you uncle joey for being the person you were. Thank you for the long talks, the loud laughs, the good memories, For giving me something to hold onto and for showing me how to appreciate."

I did it. I made it through the whole eulogy. When I got back to my seat however, I lost it. I pulled my shirt over my eyes and cried quietly as we celebrated the life of my uncle Joey. My confirmation was in a few weeks and it sucked not being able to share the day with him. In some ways maybe I still could. As I prepared for the big day I wanted to talk to God. I mean truly talk to him. I sat in my room and our conversation began. "God, I would like to take a minute to thank you for always being there for me. I didn't always believe but you did. You believed in me and that's why I've made it this far. So, once I make my confirmation I promise to dedicate the rest of my life to you." He responded through my priest at the time.

At the rehearsal, my religion class and I did confession. My priest is awesome, he has a polish accent and he preaches with his heart in his hand. When I sat down with him he said "There she is, my pride and joy. Your dedication to your faith hasn't gone unnoticed. I see that God has been shining through you." I thanked him for his kind words and I was deeply touched. I struggled with my faith for the past couple years so it felt nice to hear that. I never truly gave up on God, I just struggled in finding him.

I went home that day feeling like a million bucks. Something about confession gives me a born again feeling. I am relieved of my sins and now my mind is fully clear. I focused all my attention on Confirmation. For me, confirmation meant that I could fully accept God into my heart as I had never done before. I can build our relationship stronger and hopefully follow the path he paved for me. I could hardly wait.

The next morning I woke up and saw the sun shinning through my window. I poured myself a cup of coffee and a bowl of cereal. It was going to be a great day. After the ceremony I invited family and close friends to celebrate. Not only did we celebrate myself getting confirmed, we celebrated everyone invited for being apart of my journey. I was excited for it all.

My family and I arrived at the church and I swear it never looked so beautiful. The church was decorated and the sun glistened through the windows. I sat down in my reserved aisle and took it all in. I asked Mrs. Millano to come to the church and surely she did. When I went up to speak I felt Uncle Joey grab my hand, to calm my nerves. He was there with me, I know so. I said each word like it was a habit. It came easy, naturally.

I walked back to my seat and saw my mom and other family tearing up. It was an emotional day and we all felt it. We were called up one by one with our sponsors to get blessed. My sponsor was Jack's wife. She was always super sweet to me and I always thought of her like a second grandma. It was a special moment for the both of us. As mass ended I walked to the back of the church to greet Mrs.Millano and her daughter. It was really important to me that she was there for the big day. She was never just a teacher to me, she was someone I could come to for anything and I appreciated that. I always will.

My family and I headed back to the house as we waited for our guests to arrive. The most important people in my life showed up that day. My aunt came with Aunt Tiny, I was overjoyed that the both of them came. My aunt because at the time she was someone I looked up to, someone I wa very close with. My aunt Tiny and I were building up a relationship, I always wanted her in my life. Coach B came with his fiance and daughter, their my hockey family. Coach B believed in me from the first day he met me. He was the very reason I believed in myself. My other Coach came as well. She was the life of the party. When she walked in she handed me money, no card because she just likes to get right to the point. We had a little heart to heart moment when I thanked her for always pushing me to be my best and motivating me to "Just keep swimming." She always said those words to me. Somehow it always helped. She walked into the kitchen where everyone was sitting. She told stories of how when I first started hockey I always complained about skating which is very true. In came my dad, my stepmom and my brothers.

Mostly everyone I wanted here, was here. My God father wasn't able to make it but I knew he was proud of me and that he loved me. My God mother however, didn't show and I didn't hear from her. Our relationship was a little rocky but I still hoped she would come. My aunt Jane came with a big pot of rice. We all love her rice and she was a very Godly woman. She always instilled the grace of God in my life.

I have amazing people in my life. Everyone at that party had supported me through the hardest year of my life. I felt so loved by everyone in the room. We all shared stories while enjoying the delicious food in front of us. I have a lot to be grateful for and sometimes I forget that. That day I realized that I am so blessed. To all the wonderful people in my life and to God, thank you for that beautiful day.

School went on as it always did and the year came to an end. The last day of school was hard because that meant I had to say goodbye to Mrs. Millano. I gave her a million hugs and told her that I would miss her deeply over the summer but I was happy that I could take another break from school. Besides it was time to celebrate my sweet sixteen.

It was the day before my birthday and even though I was turning sixteen, I still wanted my family over for a party. I was excited to see everyone. Especially my aunt. My good friend and I were out to eat and I was telling her that a close friend of mine had been treating me poorly for a couple years now. This friend, he's been around since I was little and we grew up together. He lived just a door down. Lately, something changed. He hit me whenever I joked around or whenever he was mad.

It wasn't like it hurt because he's always been a soft hitter. I still hope he never gets into a fight because boy would that be a loss on his part.

He wasn't a good friend anymore, he wasn't the same person I ran around the neighborhood with or played mini sticks with. Last year he dealt with a pretty big heartbreak and so I could understand that he turned himself off. That maybe he just didn't care anymore. I couldn't deal with him always kicking me out of his house, always pushing me, making fun of me. This new me, she didn't want this negative energy around her. There's only one problem, letting go of him would be like letting go of a piece of my childhood. I was undecided and so I went to my go to.

At dinner I texted my aunt and let her know what has been going on. Usually she helped me decide what to do. Usually, she made me feel better. Times have changed. Her responses were unlike her, they were mean and hurtful. She was always hard on me and like I said she didn't sugar coat things. That day I saw a different side of her, I recall her saying, "your the idiot for staying with him, I should hit you." I felt my stomach twist and I teared up. Taking a sip of my water and clearing my throat, I responded "I came to you for help, not this." Tears streamed down my face.

My friend looking at me in awe said "Just breathe, she's being tough on you like she always is." This was a new kind of tough. The phone rung and I swear my stomach dropped to the floor. I answered and I tried to hold back the tears as I walked outside of the restaurant. I some how knew that I would end up tears. I don't remember what she said but I remember how she said it. Something about her words made me cry because when I walked back in that restaurant, I was almost speechless. My friend asked what happened and I could hardly breathe, let alone talk. So, we left and she drove me home.

I forgot about it a few hours later. I was preparing for my party the next day. I knew there was something I should do before I turned sixteen. I knew or rather I realized, I needed to cut him out of my life. It was hard, he's been my friend since I was little. He lived down the street, he went to my school. I knew it had to be done and so that's what I did. I cut him out with one text. One text in which he didn't respond to and one text I later found out, he laughed at. He didn't care about our friendship, he didn't care about anything but himself. A weight was lifted off my shoulders that day. A weight I carried around for too long.

I woke up in the morning and I was more than excited to see my family. As I was getting ready my aunt texts me to tell me she's not coming. It wasn't because she was busy and couldn't make it, it was because she didn't want to come while she was still mad at me. My makeup was streaming down my face as tears hit the floor. If she didn't come, I would never forget it. For me, turning a new age is like a fresh start. I didn't want to start it off mad and unhappy. I wanted to ring in the new age with my aunt, with my person.

My tears quickly dried when I heard that my uncle Don was coming. He has really recovered from his traumatizing experience. He's stronger than ever and I couldn't wait to see him. I took off the ruined makeup and as my stepmom like to call it, I put a new face on. Whenever I go somewhere with my step mom and she still has to get ready she always says something like "Hold on, I don't have my face on yet." She's hilarious and very beautiful. In that moment all I was worried about was getting ready on time. The guests are just about to arrive.

Hair is done, makeup is on and I had a blue romper with a white cardigan on. Most of my family had arrived, my uncle don, others aunts and uncles, cousins, and now we were waiting on my dad, my stepmom, and the kids. Most of the time they show up fashionably late. I went to go change the music when I received a message from my aunt, "I'm coming with your dad." Here comes the butterflies. My stomach was twisting and turning like when you go down a huge hill on a rollercoaster.

I saw them coming up to the front door and when I heard the doorbell ring I slowly made my way to open the door. I saw my stepmom first. She was wearing a grey and white maxi dress which she looked stunning in, and then in came my dad and my very handsome brothers. I knew my aunt would be coming shortly after so I hid behind the door. I was so nervous I actually hid behind the door. She came in and gave me a big hug and apologized. Now the party really began and the butterflies went away. My aunt said she wanted to give me my present in private.

We went to the computer room and I sat in the old, black chair and she sat on the piano bench. I notice her take a deep breath as she began to say, "Listen, I know I'm hard on you and I'm goona work on that. I just don't want you to give up." She pulled out my present and continued, "When I was going through a hard time I red this. It pulled me out of some tough times and so I want to give it to you and hopefully it will help you through your hard times" A tear fell upon her cheek and I was speechless. My aunt is one tough cookie. She has been through alot in her day. When her mom tragically passed when she was around my age, everyone said she was the strongest one. She didn't cry much, she held it together. To see her tear up was a huge moment for the both of us.

I leaned over and gave her a hug and thanked her for the meaningful gift. Im sure she knows how much it meant to me. This moment showed me she cared and that she was still in there. She very strong. Without even knowing her, if you look at her and I mean truly look at her, you would see that her strength, it comes from experiences. I don't know what it's like to lose a parent, thank God, but I can see how it has affected my family. My dad never healed from losing his mom. You can see that just by looking at him. He never healed and I don't blame him. I don't think my aunt ever healed either. I think that she has moved forward but I think that dealing with the loss of a parent, it takes time. I look at my dad and his siblings with the utmost respect. They lost their mother, and they still turned out to be amazing people. Beautiful people, they don't just happen.

That day was a day to remember. Before I could open presents and blow out the candles, my aunt had to go. I walked her and my other aunt out to the car and just before I closed the door my aunt said, "I'll never give up on you." I replied sarcastically, "You already almost did." As she giggled and responded, "but I didn't." I closed the car door and as I walked back to this house I looked back, realizing I just found my security.

I felt secure in my aunt and in her words. "I will never give up on you." Those words were huge to me. So many people have left my life. They walk in and out when they choose because I let it happen. For her to say those words, allowed me to fully and truly trust her. I loved my aunt and the friendship that we had.

As summer sun became hotter, the fun had just begun. It was July, already halfway through summer. It's crazy how quickly time goes by. One day we're babies learning how to talk, read, and write and the next we're in highschool figuring out what to do for the rest of our lives. My aunt and I were on a little bit of a rocky road. It has now been a few days since I've heard from her. That doesn't seem like much but for us it is. We talk everyday. The last time we talked we were fighting about how she doesn't say I love you back. Which I understand she's not a mushy person but it was like I had to beg for three words.

Looking back at this fight, it wasn't really about my aunt and what she said or didn't say. It was about validation. I struggled with it. The fight ended with both parties upset. Since he fight, she hasn't responded to my texts. I wasn't sure what was going on, we fight all the time and never have we not spoken. So, to make sure she was okay I texted her sister and asked if she knew anything. She said, "I just talked to her on the phone, seems fine to me."

I was worried but there wasn't much I could do. Then, I received the most heartbreaking text. My aunt told me we both needed to take time to grow and reflect. She had been dealing with a head injury for years now. She finished to say that for now she didn't want to be apart of my life and that I had to much drama and personal issues. I didn't move.

A wave came crashing at the shore, A pin dropped to the floor, as a moment of silence filled my bedroom. I finished reading those last words and suddenly I couldn't move. Then, it came. I cried so hard I was screaming. An instant sharp feeling came through my chest. My heart hurt. I couldn't stop crying. I just lost my person, and more importantly I just lost my aunt. This was by far the most painful thing I had ever felt. My mom came rushing in to see what was wrong and as I told her, veins popped out of her head. After comforting me, she went outside to smoke a cigarette. I thought about what I was going to say back. I didn't have it in my heart to lash out and say something equally hurtful. That's just not who I am.

My grandma raised me to have a pure heart and to love with the best intentions. I replied, "I understand, I will always be here if you need anything." This was not easy for me at all. I felt lost. Another one of my aunts had done something similar a couple years back and this aunt knew that. I was so sick of people leaving me. My stepmom was already on her way when I got this text. When she pulled up my mom told her everything. I held back the tears and said "It's done, it's over with." As we headed inside to get my stuff my mom said, "It hurt me to hear the text and it wasn't even towards me,"

It would hurt anyone to hear that, I'm sure. For some reason, I feel like I saw it coming. People always leave, I just wish she wasn't one of them. At my dads, my pain was quickly relieved by my brothers as they comforted me with love. Good thing my stepmom came when she did because who knows, I could've ended up back in the hole I was in before.

As a teenager, it's hard to control your emotions. Teenagers can be overdramatic, that's just the way it is. For me to keep calm and think rationally in that moment instead of raging out, was a big step and showed maturity. It was hard to calm myself enough to control how I reacted in the situation. If I would've said something harsh, moments later when all was said and done, I would regret it. The car ride to my dad's was like the rubble that's left after a fire. I had to decide what to do with the cards I was dealt. It wasn't easy.

Chapter 6 THE AWAKENING

In the blink of an eye, all of it disappeared. All the issues I was dealing with suddenly didn't matter because this day was the day I could've died, and that changed everything. It cleared my slate. Maybe I did die but instead I was born again and this was my second shot at life.

July 30th, 2016, I will ever forget you, you are the date I carry with me everyday, amongst others. I was on my way to my dad's camp and I was reading a book that I had only been a few days into. Isn't it great when you read a book that you just can't seem to put down? You're so intrigued by the story line that you wish it wouldn't end. I wish I never put down the book. We arrived at my dad's camp and I went straight to the little wooden table in the backyard near the woods and close to the unlit fire. I kept reading til my brother and my cousin went for a ride on my dad's Atv's. I jumped at the chance, I love the adrenaline.

We were off and the sun was shining through the trees. It was beautiful outside, I've always loved the skies after a rain storm. It was raining the few days prior so it was really muddy. There's something about the way the skies clear and the sun comes out just before it sets,

I love the color of the sky. We did a few laps around the little lake that laid at the bottom of a huge hill on my dad's land. We smelled food and rushed back to eat. While I was eating, I kept reading my book. I saw my brother and my cousin going for another ride and ran to meet them. It was getting dark so I knew it would be my last chance to go.

Our engines were rubbing and we were going fast as usual. The sun was down and it as barely light outside. My cousin and my brother stopped in the middle of the woods to go look for places to put their tree stand. That was the last thing I remembered for a long time. I just remembered sitting there looking at all the trees blowing in the wind. I looked at all nature had to offer. The tree's were ruffling and the mud just beginning to dry up. If I had only known, If I had just went back to camp, If I didn't go for one more ride. Would it have happened?

From the stories I was told and the memory I regained, what happened next was the best and worst thing that could've ever happened to me. My brother and my cousin returned and we headed back to camp. On the way back, I was trying to catch up to them when I started to lose them, I picked my head up and looked for them when suddenly an old tree branch hit me in the neck. I blacked out. I was still driving and steering. I steered off the dirt road and went downhill through more trees and brush. Still on the Atv and still unconscious, I finally crashed into a tree. I was still on the Atv and when I woke up I fell on the ground. Unbelievably, I gathered myself and walked back to the trailer. There's no way possible I walked back by myself. All the trauma and Injuries, there's no way. I think I had a guardian angel with me. I didn't walk alone.

I was wearing a grey tank top and a white sweatshirt which was drenched in blood. My step mom saw me and in shock, called for my mom. "Andrea's hurt!" She yelled. I made it inside the trailer home and everyone rushed to greet me. I was sitting on a little chair when my mom with a shaky voice said, "What's that sticking out of her arm?" My dad quickly examined the spot and said "It's a twig." He asked my brother to get pliers so he could remove it. He pulled it out of my arm, ouch.

My neck was swollen and blood kept flowing out of it. My dad looked at it and said "She has to go to the hospital." My little brother, who's 14 and just about the best teenage brother I could ask for, my mom, my moms best friend and I quickly hopped in the car.

We arrived at the creepiest hospital any of us had ever seen. There was no one around and the light were flickering. Talk about a horror movie scene. We finally found a staff member that assisted us. I needed stitches, that was a given, The wounds were so dirty and needed to be cleaned out. They stitched me up, 15 stitches.

The doctor came in to talk to my mom and said something like "We've done all we could for her here but because of the swelling in her neck, she needs to go the children's hospital, by ambulance." My neck was so swollen it looked like I was six hundred pounds.This was when I really woke up. From the time I was sitting in the woods on the Atv to this very moment in the hospital. Everything else was a complete blur. My little brother came in after my stitches, gave me a kiss on my forehead and a mint. Just barely awake I asked my mom "What happened?" She replied, "stop playing, you know what happened."

Moments later I asked again, "Mom, what happened to me?" "You just asked me that, stop it." Only I wasn't kidding I didn't remember a thing. As I waited to go in the ambulance, one thing came to mind. Would I ever play hockey again? I still didn't know the extent of my injuries. The doctor came in to tell me it was time to go. My mom and her best friend said goodbye and gathered their things. As I was transported to the second hospital, my mom had to go back to camp to drop off my brother and pack our things.

On the way to the second hospital I tried to think of what just happened. I couldn't remember anything and that's what scared me the most. How could I not remember a thing? My mind felt full like I had a million things on my mind but really I just had one thing. What the heck just happened to me. It felt like I fell asleep because I completely blacked out. Everyone said I was awake but again I couldn't remember the rest of the ride. I woke up in the hospital bed with my mom and her best friend sitting to the side.

The doctors diagnosed my injuries with a cervical sprain. They further explained I would need to wear a neck brace. I was glad that it wasn't worse. All I can remember is that I really needed to pee. It was very painful. I felt a shocking pain shoot up from my back to my neck. Ouch. My mom helped me get on my feet and I walked to the bathroom on my own. It hurt just to sit down. I was shaking holding on to the sidebar and I swear I must've peed for ten minutes straight. The walk back to my room was equally painful. Every twist, turn, even the slightest move was excruciatingly painful. Having this neck brace on was going to be not only uncomfortable but very painful.

The neck brace definitely meant no hockey. The one thing I looked forward to, and that also meant I wouldn't see the one person who can cheer me up. I couldn't finish Coach's clinic and I was so upset. I sat in my hospital bed thinking about what just happened. I could've died or ended up paralyzed and I didn't. I'm so lucky, I got a second chance at life. Who saved me though? There's no way I miraculously made it out. God, he saved me. How can I be so sure?

The night of my accident, I had a sterling silver, cross necklace on. As I previously stated my shirt and sweatshirt were covered in blood from my chin to my waist, I was covered. My necklace however, didn't have a single drop of blood on it. To this day I rarely ever take it off.

It saved me and it's the reason I'm still here today. When I finally got discharged I was more than happy to go home and see my grandparents.

The ride home sucked. Every bump, turn, and stop, flinched my body and I felt excruciating pain. I was counting the minutes till we got home. My mom, the amazing person that she is, helped me out of the car which wasn't easy. I slowly but surely made my way to the front step. Home sweet home. I opened the door and saw my older sister sitting on the steps, tearing up as I made my way to the couch. Which she still won't admit. I sat down and again more pain. My sister is awkward in these situations. I find it funny. She didn't really know what to say so she just sat there looking at me for a few moments.

My phone was blowing up. I texted my sister to let her know what happened. She responded immediately and drove to my house. I looked awful. I looked worse than what it was, the neckbrace didn't help much. When she arrived she sat beside me on the couch. She asked the usual, "Are you okay?" I wanted to respond sarcastically but I didn't. She went on to tell me about her prom and showed me pictures of her and her date. She looked so pretty in her black dress and her hair pulled up. She only stayed for a little while when she said her parents were waiting outside. I got off the couch and walked outside, even though I looked like I got hit by a car. I walked slowly to her mom where I received a gently hug. She looked at me and struggled to hold back the tears like my mom did during my depression.

As they pulled out of my driveway, I looked back. That would be the last time I would see my sister. As a result of my accident I had very little movement in my arms but I could still text. I texted Coach notifying her that I was done for the season. She wanted to know what happened. I went on to tell her I really want to see her, she replied "What hospital?" I answered "I'm home now." "Good because I hate hospitals, I'll swing by when I can." I then texted my other coach, Coach B. He's an amazing guy and he's done so much for me. Without him, I wouldn't be playing hockey and I wouldn't believe in myself. He has always supported me through everything even if it wasn't hockey. He's my hockey dad. When he found out about my accident he didn't hesitate to come see me.

He had just had a baby, a beautiful little girl. He came by and It was so good to see him. He brought the baby who I hadn't met yet. My coach is a funny guy. He was cracking jokes and even the baby thought it was funny. After he left, I realized how much he cares about me as a person and not just as a hockey player. My hockey dad.

My first shower since the accident absolutely sucked. The worst part of the accident was that I couldn't shower alone, so my mom helped me. Talk about an invasion of privacy. For two weeks she had to shower me. What a great summer. If I couldn't shower on my own, imagine all of the other things I couldn't do. I couldn't even wipe my own ass. To say that me and my mom are close is an understatement. Before my accident, my mom schedule a counseling session. I didn't want to miss it, after all a few days ago I could've been dead.

I was definitely going.The car ride was a little easier but the pain was still unbearable. When we arrived I took a good look around and headed in. My counselor greeted us with the utmost grace. This counselor was very easy to talk to. She had this way about her, this way of understanding without overstepping. It was nice to have someone really hear me out. When all was said and done, she looked at me like I had untapped potential. As I got out of my chair and headed out, She gently gave me hug and wished me a speedy recovery.

On the way home, one very special person popped in my mind. My aunt. We still weren't on the best of terms but I let her know the night after the accident. It didn't change anything but I still missed her. It was different this time around, this time when I was thinking about her, I asked myself; is it time to give up? Then, I remembered my aunt

Tiny's words. "The ball is in her court." Yeah, the ball is in her court, I've done just about everything I could at this point. The rest is up to her. That gave me relief and I realized the what I hadn't realized all this time, She will come around in due time.

The next few days, I started to get a little more movement in my arms and I finally fed myself. Often times, people take for granted the simplest things in life. When were born, for most people it's a given that we walk and talk on our own, and overtime we feed and shower ourselves. For some people, that's not a possibility. There's people on this planet who need help doing everyday things. This accident taught me to appreciate the little things, I appreciate the fact that I can do my hair and my makeup, I appreciate the fact that I can eat and shower on my own. To all those who suffer from this daily struggle, I understand you and I pray for you. I made a special thank you to my greatest friend, God. God, thank you for allowing me to have the little things in life. I know that it's a privilege, not a guarantee.

Everyday I healed a little more and I got back to some type of normalcy. One day I woke up and heard the birds chirping. I went outside and I felt the sun on my face. It had been so long since the last time I felt it. Two years to be exact. One day I woke up, and it was there. Two years later I woke up, and it was gone. My phone buzzed and it was my Coach. She was letting me know that she would be over soon. As a smile was brought to my face, I opened my book, the book I was reading before my accident. I was on the final pages when I heard a loud voice.

It was just my coach talking to my grandpa. She sat outside on the deck with me. It was so good to see her. Through the past couple years, She became my mentor. She became the person that would be there from the very beginning to the bittersweet end. She just cracks me up. She began to tell me a few stories which made me laugh left and right. Then she asked "What are we doing for college?" I replied, "I want to be in the fashion industry and I'm gonna try to double major with writing." She was one of the very few people who encouraged me to follow my dreams no matter what they were. She shook her head and smiled as she continued to make me laugh.

After what felt like two minutes but was really a half hour, She headed out. I don't think she realized how much it meant to me that she came by. It reassured me that she does care about me. She's a very hard person to read but I think I was getting the hang of it. I looked up at the sun after she left, I watched it glisten between the clouds. I sat on my back deck and thought about life for sometime before I got too hot and went in.

There was something unusual about that day. It was one of the happy days. I was calm and this was the first day I didn't feel any pain. Not a single ounce. I sat back down and kept watching the olympics. Today was a good day. This was the day I realized that all I need is somewhere to call home, a friend who listens, and something to believe in. I had all four. God, that's who I believe in. After all this time, I finally figured it out. He was building me up not tearing me down. He was showing me that life is going to take strength, he was showing me that you have to believe that one day it will get better.

Ever since my Coach visited I felt calm. For the next few days I sat on my back deck and watched the trees blow in the wind. It was so peaceful. The sun was at it's highest point in the sky. I couldn't believe how different I felt since the day of my accident. I looked up to the sky and I watched the clouds move. What a life changer.

This accident it wasn't a tragedy. It was a miracle. It was my miracle and it was God's way of telling me, I'm here and I always have been. I don't know why I ever doubted him, If I had known that this is what it felt like to let him in, I would've never let him go. God, I want to thank you for never giving up on me. Without you I wouldn't be here so I owe you another thank you. A huge thank you, for saving my life.

Sometimes I ponder about the mysteries of life. Why was I do lucky? Why did I make it out when others weren't so lucky? Now I knew that I had a purpose. God wants me down here for a reason. A huge part of me died that day. The part of me that thought I couldn't live without my aunt. The part of me that thought all life has to offer was hurt and tragedy. The depressed part of me, it was left in that day. From here on out, I'm going to be the best me that I can be.

Chapter 7 My Life Since

Things are so clear now. I look out my window and I see a world of opportunity. I was at my lowest point for such a long time and now it was like nothing could stand in my way. I felt like a huge weight was lifted off my shoulders. The summer sun was still bright and it was hot as ever. My neck brace was finally off after having it on for two weeks, which doesn't seem like a long time until you're the one wearing it. I felt rejuvenated. There's no way I could possibly explain exactly what this felt like.

For a while I closed off the thought of ever feeling this happy again. I lost hope and I was just about done trying to save myself. The thing is, I was giving in to the slapshots life was shooting at me, I was going to let them win. Only I was taught differently. My Coach has taught me lessons far beyond what lies in the rink. She has taught me that even at your lowest point you can get back up to reach an even higher point.

God agreed and so I think through this accident he was trying to tell me that I can't give up and I definitely need to listen up. My relationship with God has greatly improved. One thing I've noticed is that since I've opened my heart and ears to God, I felt much more alive.

The accident wasn't far behind me but I was recovering faster than expected. I felt great and I was ready to start getting back to doing summer activities before I had to go back to school.

My dad was throwing a little family get together for my grandma's birthday at his house. At this point my stitches were out and already turning into scars so I was surely going to be there. I wondered if my aunt was going to be there.

Our relationship is still rocky and I still wasn't ready to fully and truly have her back in my life. I asked her if she was going and luckily she said that she couldn't make it. I think that we both needed time and there was no way I was ready to see her face to face or even talk to her about what had happened prior to my accident.

Whenever I thought of my aunt I thought about what I would say to her if we were to ever have the talk that we needed to have. Would I tell her how absolutely heartbroken I was or would I put up a front like I didn't care at all. Losing her was still hard on me.

Throughout life, the hardest thing I've ever had to do was grieve the loss of a person that was still very much alive. It was frustrating to miss her because there was nothing I could do about it. It felt like she passed away but only it was worse. It's not that she couldn't talk to me, it's that she didn't want to and for a long time, I let that rip me apart. The accident though, it changed all that.

I was no longer grieving and for a while she didn't even cross my mind. Maybe I was focused on my recovery or maybe I was so tired of missing her that one day I just gave up. I love my aunt and I always will, she knows that, I know that. Will I miss her? That was the real question.

I think I missed our relationship more than I missed her. Sine the day of my accident all I wanted was for her to find all that she was looking for. I think for the longest time since her head injury she was looking for peace. So that's what I prayed for. I prayed that one day, everything in her life would work out as she wanted to, I prayed that one day she could have all she ever wanted.

I want the best for her and all my family. I think that life is too hard and things get too complicated. We all deserve an equal opportunity at having a time in our life where we are happy and healthy. That's what I will always want for her. No matter how far we grow apart, no matter how much she changes. I will always be here for her and I will never stop praying for her.

My accident taught me that everybody needs someone that's betting on them. Everybody needs that somebody who is hoping and praying that they will make the best of what they've got. I had so many people rooting for me and so I've decided, I'm gonna root for her.

It was time for the party at my dad's house. This was the first time I got all done up for something since my accident. It was a little difficult. Doing my hair was hard because my arms started to ache and my neck was screaming stop every time I tilted it. I didn't say anything because I wanted to do things on my own again.

My makeup didn't hurt so much. I was all ready to go and it was a beautiful day out. It was one of those days where the sun is in the sky at just the right spot and the temperature isn't too hot or too cold. The breeze was slight but yet still moving. It was one of those days.

When we arrived at the party everyone seemed so excited to see me. First person I hugged was my stepmom. I love getting to spend time with her, she always treated me like her own kid and that was a special thing for me. Then I hugged everyone else one by one. My little brother jumped on me which at first hurt but his hands are healing. Babies hands, they have their own way of healing wounds that isn't medically possible.

Family time, it was just what I needed. It was great to see my dad's side of the family because I don't get to see them all that often. They're all great people just like my dad. He was cooking up hamburgers and hotdogs when I went to give him a big hug. We're really close now and in most ways I look up to him. He is one strong dude. He gave me a big and of course cracked a joke.

I ran over to my grandma and gave her a hug and a kiss. She looked different that day. She looked extra beautiful, extra vibrant and definitely more happy than usual. I don't think it was because it was her birthday. I think she was enjoying being around the family just as much as I was. The sun continued to shine. The way the light was glistening on my dad's glace table reminded me of the way Gods light. It's always on, sometimes you just have to dial it up.

We sung to my grandma as she blew out the candles. Suddenly and unexpectedly she began to cry. She then explained that she really appreciated everyone spending time with her and that she doesn't get to see all of us as much as she wants to. She thanked my dad and stepmom for hosting the party and for taking such good care of her as she wiped up the tears.

My dad has a huge heart. He cares for family so deeply and I really admire that part of him. My stepmom is amazing but one thing she's great at is being there for everyone else. She's the first person any of us call if we need anything. She's the heart and soul of the family. She gives her all to each and everyone one of my dad's kids and that amazes me everyday.

It was a great day, definitely one to remember. On my way home I watched the sun go down just outside my window. The way home was a breeze. My neck was aching but for a moment I didn't mind. After all, I didn't want to let one little thing ruin my day.

When summer comes to an end it's both sad and exciting. At the end of each summer I usually do something fun with my friends but at this point I didn't really have any. My friend and I grew apart faster than I would've thought. My best friend Khloe wasn't really apart of my life and again I was stuck at a crossroad.

This summer was hard not because of the accident but because I dealt with so much loss. The loss of my aunt, all of my friends, and the loss of a part of me. That's where my friend Kylie comes in. She was one of the very few people that visited me during my accident and got me out of the house.

We became close when my uncle passed and her mom got into a car accident. It was weird how fast we bonded and it taught me something. You don't need to be part of a big group of friends. You only need God. What you want is to be apart of a crowd and for me this friendship was all I wanted.

She's someone I feel like I can trust and someone that understands me. It's just different, I can't trust her as much as I want to because like I said my door is always open. People come and go when they please.

It's emotionally draining to feel like you constantly have to have your guard up. One thing I've learned is that I can trust God. Since he's been around, he has become my guard. He has stopped everything from hurting me. When you let God into your heart, there's no way of knowing how his light will shine through you.

A couple weeks before school started, Coach had a field hockey game at my high school. I haven't seen her since she last visited and I knew it would be good to see her. My cousin Vanessa was over and she always liked Coach so it was perfect timing.

I was excited to not only see Coach but to get ready. Any chance I get to get ready is huge for me. A couple weeks ago I couldn't even go to the bathroom on my own and now look at me. My cousin had to help me with my hair but I was still making great progress.

When we arrived at the field, I was listening in to see if I could hear Coach's voice. Surely, I did. It brought a smile to my face, I missed that loud voice of hers. Vanessa and I watched the game laughing at how crazy Coach gets during it. She gets so intense so quickly.

After the game we walked across the field. I saw Coach and gave her a hug. We shared a few laughs which is always expected. It felt good to see her. She complimented me, "you look pretty". After I thanked her I was thinking that happy must look good on me. I am genuinely happy.

We chatted only for a little while. We both walked away and as she left I looked back once more symbolizing a very significant moment in my life. The moment I realized what it meant to be happy.

It didn't mean that everything in life was going as I pictured it. It meant that with the cards I've been dealt, I was playing a new game. A game where I wasn't gambling away every part of me for just a hint of happiness. In this game happiness wasn't the prize, it was the player.

Summer was ending and now I have to prepare myself for the hardest year, academically. Junior year is the biggest year in anyone's high school career. SATs, college visits, and one very important decision.

What do you want to do for the rest of your life? Who do you want to be? That's the question I get asked on a daily basis. As teens in this day and age, were constantly under pressure. Everybody wants us to do the best with what we have to offer because we will be influencing future generations.

What if I chose the wrong path? How do I know if what I've chosen to do is what I've meant to do? I'm making a decision that will affect me for the rest of my life. Growing up I always dreamed of being a lawyer or a teacher. My dreams were constantly changing, my imagination was growing as fast as I was.

This decision took some soul searching. Over the past two years I've found that I am fascinated with fashion and art. Writing was always one of my interests. Anything that makes me use the creative side of my brain, sparks an interest in me.

I fell in love with art my freshman year. The way my hand created an image I was thinking in my brain, amazed me. Shocked me actually. It's amazing how your hands and brain work together to create something unique. My eyes saw something farther than what I could dream.

Fashion, there's just something about it. You can dress someone up and make them look like a completely different person or you can dress them down and hope that they carry themselves well enough to make it look beautiful. I love putting outfits together and last year I followed that passion.

In May before the summer had breached, I received a huge opportunity to work at the biggest fashion event within the city. I fell in love with every step. Not just the fashion aspect but creating a show that would be highly anticipated. It was about working together with a team to create a vision.

So I have to sort between fashion, writing, and art. Aren't they all the same in one way or another? They're all creative in every aspect. I'm passionate about a lot of things. I think that since I lost hockey I was looking in other areas that I could relieve stress in.

God do I miss hockey. Months before my accident I was thinking about giving it up. Not because I lost interest in it, not because I didn't think I was good enough, but because I felt as though I didn't have support. Playing hockey has always been my first love. I truly mean that.

I fell in love with every aspect. One thing that killed my passion was that I didn't have anyone there to see it. I never really had family at my games, no-one ever came out to watch. Coach B would drive me to every game and practice. He made sure I didn't give up.

It's just not the same. Whenever I played a great game I would look up to the bleachers and no-one was there to see it. I guess I always felt that if someone's passionate about something you should be there supporting them every chance you get.

Looking back, I realized that I had so much more support than I could've ever imagined. Coach B was cheering me on every game. He congratulated me every game. My teammates game me pats on the back. I had a family at hockey and I miss them. I miss every part of it.

There's always one game that comes to mind when I think of hockey. It was one where my sister and her mom and even my mom were on the bleachers and I introduced them to my friends and Coach B. My mom hadn't been to a game that season and my sister has never seen me play. I felt like it was my time to shine, it was time to deliver. Hockey is like a performance. You rehearse and you perfect your craft until showtime. The audience has given you all of their attention and now it time for you to put on a show.

It was moments before the curtain opened and I was sitting in the locker room alone thinking about how I really wanted to play the game of my life. I wanted to make my family proud, my coach and teammates included. I tried to calm my nerves and kept telling myself to give it all I've got. I put on my helmet and I buckled the straps, grabbed my stick and walked out of the locker room. It was warm up time. I spent most of the time stretching and talking to Coach B. I took a look up at the bleachers and for once I saw someone there. So this is how it feels to have support. What a great feeling knowing people are that cheering you on. They specifically came to see me and that was really huge for me. It lit a fire in my soul.

That day I played the game of my life. I play defense and to me that always meant you're not worried about yourself, you're worried about the person behind you. You're the goalies protector. The referee blew his whistle and we're all at the face off. It always gets really quiet for me. I no longer hear any voices. I take a look at all the players and at this point not a single thought crosses my mind. I patiently wait for the ref to drop the puck and with one quick motion he did.

We were off. It was a fast pace game and the players were fairly skilled. I kept looking up at the bleachers because I was so happy they came. I had a lot of energy. The puck was loose down at the other end when a player from the other team came and picked it up. As a defensemen, I always stayed back because I didn't think I was fast enough backwards. Now it was just me and her, I was all that stood in the way between her and the goalie I had my head up, knees bent and easily I snatched the puck as the buzzer went off.

The team huddled and Coach B said his famous words "Good job everybody." Every game he said that, win or lose. He's a great coach because no matter what, as long as we were happy with ourselves, he would be happy too. The ref blew his whistle and we lined up. Second period was a breeze. Third period however was hectic. One of the other team's best players stood at the top of the big red circles on the ice and lined up to take a slap shot. When she shot I saw the puck going straight for the net and I stood right in front of it.

Ouch. I fell straight to the ground but I saved it and that was more important. My good friend and the coaches daughter, came over and said "you alright kid?" I replied, "Just dandy." She helped me back up and I sat on the bench. Coach B looked at me giggling and said "what're ya doing standing in front of a shot like that?" I looked at him with a smile and said, "I'd rather have the puck hit me than the back of the net." He shaked his head and went back to watching the game.

We lost but it was a moral victory for me. After the game, my sister ran up to me and gave me a hug. I could tell she was worried. She asked "are you okay?" I responded, "Yeah, I'm fine" She wiped off the makeup that ran down my face during the game. Her mom gave me a hug as well. I thanked them for coming and said my goodbye as I walked to the locker room. I looked back and saw my sister look back too. I didn't think anything of it until now. That was pretty special to me.

I will always have the memory of hockey with me. Even if I never play again, it will always have a special place in my heart. For me to understand that for awhile I would have to let go of hockey, was really hard on me. I don't think I ever came to terms with it. That's one thing the accident took away. It took away my happy place and more importantly, it took away a big part of my soul. I believe that being a hockey player has changed my soul.

So has the accident though. My soul has always been broken. Hockey filled holes but it never fully put the pieces back together. God finished the puzzle. Since the accident, I opened my soul to him and everyday he worked on the puzzle. It turns out he made a beautiful picture. All that was left was the place where hockey went.

It's funny, we don't realize how lucky we are until we lose something. It took alot for me to realize that no matter what, I should never give up on things that I'm passionate about. Now I know that I never will. This year ahead would be challenging because I didn't have my stress reliever but I do have God and I believe that he will be the one that takes all my worries. I believe that he'll help me accomplish things I never thought I could.

Junior year, yikes. I couldn't believe how fast everything was going. It felt like just yesterday I was a freshman walking into a nightmare. Now I'm a junior walking into the stressful year. One things for sure, I couldn't wait to see Mrs. Milano. I was ready and as long as God is with me, this year would be my year. Now it's time to deliver, only as a student instead of hockey player. Showtime.

Chapter 8 ROAD TO RECOVERY

I woke up extra early, I wanted to look my best. Nobody really knew about the accident and I didn't really care to tell them. My friend Kylie asked me to meet her at one of our favorite teachers room. The first day of school is like a meet and greet. You meet your new teachers and greet your old friends. This year however, my friends from past years were no longer apart of my life. I lost them in the midst of it all. Truthfully, that didn't really cross my mind.

This new me believes that if I've got God, a place to call home, a friend to turn to, and inspiration then I was going to be just fine. When I met up with Kylie, we went to go look for our lockers. First, we made a pit stop. Mrs. Milanos room of course. I popped my head in and said "where's my favorite teacher?" She looked up with a smile. We were catching up when the announcements came on to state that all classes would start late. Kylie and I looked at eachother smiling, knowing we had sometime to mess around. We walked around for a half hour, laughing and reminiscing about summer and all that we did. The first day of school is a breeze. What we didn't know but would soon figure out is that this year would keep us on our toes.

I stopped in my old art teachers room to grab the projects I left from the year prior. She asked, "Do you have any free periods?" I replied, "Yep. Second, third, and ninth. Why?" "I need a mentor for my special education class, would you be interested? It's third period." "Yeah of course."

I didn't really need three study halls so I figured it'd be a great experience. I didn't really think about it, it was an impulse decision. I never thought that mentoring this class would change me and my whole entire perspective on life. Along with this class I started teaching second grade religion at my church. When God told me I had a purpose, he didn't exactly tell me what my purpose was. I don't think anyone can tell you, I think you have to learn all on your own.

That's what I really focused on since the day of my accident. God kept me here for a reason. I decided that I was going to put all my energy towards figuring it out. The hard part was trying to figure out whether I was headed in the direction God intended for me or I was making making a wrong turn. That's just it. I'm not suppose to know, that's what life's all about. It's not about the destination, it's about the choices you didn't make an the ones you did. It's about the obstacles you overcome.

I spent the first part of junior year focused and determined. My grades were awesome and I had a good head on my shoulders. My classes were hard but I was up for the challenge. My hardest class was drawing and painting. I was in a funk. As an artist, I wasn't putting my heart into my work. I didn't feel motivated. I felt stuck. What I needed was inspiration and quick. My grade was declining rapidly and I was struggling to get it back up.

Inspiration is defined in so many ways. Whether it's the sky or the way the trees blow in the wind. Everybody has something that inspires them. For me, it wasn't something, it was someone or rather a lot of someones. My inspiration was staring me in the eyes and for a long time I didn't open my heart to let it in. How could I not see it? I'm surrounded by inspiration.

My third period class inspires me. Now that I've met these amazing kids, I can't believe how much they've opened my heart. I can't believe how much they've taught me.

I believe that things like this are meant to happen. Slowly but surely God's plan for me is unraveling. The way he put his heart into these kids eyes was incredibly life changing. I saw how he worked through each and every one of them.

They're amazing people because although life hasn't been easy for them they put one foot in front of the other and they made their way through life. They showed me that no matter what life throws at you, take it and make it great. Put your heart into everything you do and don't, not even for a second, look back.

I carry their stories with me everyday. I guess this year that's what every became about. It wasn't about what I had been through, it was about what I've learned from it and what I'm going to do with it.

I spent too much time focusing on what I had to do to make it to tomorrow, I missed the beautiful things that live in today. I just wasn't living until now. Now, I'm awake.

Everyday I count my blessings. Even on the hard days I think, what about today showed me that loves resides in my life. Sometimes it's hard and I struggle to come up with a list of things but there is always something to be grateful for.

My weekdays I was grateful to be able to spend time with my 3rd period friends. Yes, friends. They're my equals. They're no different from anyone on this planet. I was grateful that God put me on their journey. I was grateful that I got to share my love for art. More importantly I was grateful that I got to see another day.

My weekends I was grateful for the chance to see my little brothers. It's amazes me that I get to watch them grow. They give me the most love I've ever received and it seems like no matter what I'll always have that.

Teaching religion takes me to another level on being grateful. It's a blessing. I get to share the love I have for God. I take that knowledge and I try my best to instill it into their hearts and souls. I have always loved kids, I feel like the world can learn a lot from them.

I know I have. My junior year was primarily about taking giant leaps towards the goals I set for myself. The people I've met this year were helping me and I couldn't be anymore thankful. I can't express my gratitude in words.

With all of the support and love I received, I wanted to pay it forward and so I started a project. I wanted to make other people feel the love that I felt. So, for Christmas I celebrated by giving back.

I emailed the volunteer director of the homeless shelter closest to me. I made a proposal that stated,

"Hello,

How are you today? My name is Andrea Cottrell,

With Christmas right around the corner, I have thought about what I want for Christmas. I would like to give back. I was wondering if I could get a lot of people to donate items, could I bring it to the city mission on Christmas eve? If I'm able to do this all I would need is a list of things that are most needed, a time to bring everything, and I'll be able to spread the word.

Thank you for your time in reading this email. Please get back to me at a time most convenient for you.

God Bless!"

After a week or two we got to planning and I got to work. I wanted to make this a Christmas to remember. I started to spread the word and I received so many contributions. Mostly from my school and my church but also from people that I didn't even know. It was unforgettable, witnessing all of these people coming together to make a difference, it warmed my heart.

When it was time to bring down the items to the shelter, I was amazed. I had over 300 items. It's crazy how much you can accomplish when you put your mind to it. When my family and I were bringing all of the donations in, we saw a smile on everyone's face. Although some of them are struggling right now, they still managed to smile and that to me is the grace of God.

I was more than satisfied with myself and all of the people that donated. I found that through giving I receive. My Christmas wasn't over. I was determined to do all that I could to serve God especially during the holidays. I have a lot to be thankful for and for a while I lost sight of that. So it was time to go to God's house and praise him in all his glory.

At Christmas eve mass I volunteered to do one of the readings and one of my students volunteered to carry baby Jesus up to the altar. It was a surreal moment. I was walking side by side with my student and we both gave all of our love to the lord. I must be doing something right. I was so proud of her for stepping up as a second grader. I almost shed tears when I was walking up with her.

When it came time to do the reading, I suddenly was really nervous. As I stepped up to the podium to speak, I choked. God took my hand in that moment and showed me that in his house I will not have fear.

I am safe here and he is with me. I read through the reading with the utmost confidence and grace.

For once, I was proud of myself and the person I've become. When I got back home, everyone was proud of me too. This Christmas the house was filled with cheer as my family reunited under one house to celebrate. For a long time my family was split in half. Many years ago there was a dispute that hasn't ended till now. Everyone was together again and wow did it feel good.

Around the holidays, the world suddenly stops and in that moment you just enjoy what you have. My perspective has changed. Now I live in the moment, every moment, everyday. God saved my life and that made me live, truly live. My road to recovery has been long and hard. I look at life so differently and I can't believe how long it's been since I've felt this way.

All my struggles, pain, and hurt was leading me to here. This is what God wanted. He wanted me to see that he was building me up even when for the longest time, it felt like I was being brought down. There was still something missing. We as humans are always think about what we could have. We could be given the world and it still wouldn't be enough.

Hockey, I miss you. I miss your healing sessions. If I could never play hockey again, it's not that I wouldn't be happy, It's just that I wouldn't be me. I just wasn't finished with it. One day, we would meet again but one day felt so far away. The more pain I felt on a daily basis, the more I missed hockey. Although it couldn't take this pain away, it could take my mind off of it.

I finally felt happy and I wanted hockey to be apart of my life along with my aunt. I thought a lot about how different my life is now that she's not in it. I took a look back at all the words said. I understood where she was coming from. She wanted me to stop relying on her for answers, she wanted me to learn on my own and I wasn't upset about that. I was upset by her choice of words.

My aunt and I are so different but at the same time we're so alike. She is not at all in anyway sensitive and I definitely am. I look at it as she doesn't feel the same way about the situation as I do. I wondered if it had any effect on her. I took another step back.

I looked at my life and asked myself if I was happy. Do I need her? At this point I have built myself up so much so that it didn't really matter if she was there to see it or not. Then I paused, maybe this is what she wanted?

I opened up the bible and looked to God for the answers and surely I found them. My door is always open. If she wants to be back in my life, she was welcomed. This year was not about me and her. It was the year of self love and growth. I realized that I'm always going to want something more. That's just the thing, with age comes wisdom. I had to differentiate between my wants and needs.

God again took my hand and showed me that I have amazing people in my life. At the exact moment that I was stuck in reminiscing about my aunt and the relationship we had, my Coach texted me. We were in a deep conversation. It was one of those heart to hearts and her exact words were, "Even though God and I have decided to see other people we still talk from time to time and have each other's backs. I'm not a religious creature by nature but I do have faith and I do believe in signs and I know that you are a sign from God as well.

God works in mysterious ways Nevaeh I know that is one thing for sure in the 35 years I've been on this Earth I know for sure that he does work in mysterious ways and puts obstacles in our path to make sure that we make the right decision and if we don't make the right decision we clearly learn from the mistakes that we've made and grow from there.

Life may be too short life may be too long but there is one thing that is for certain it's the hyphen between the two dates of birth and death that you make your own nobody else just you. You will have friends that love you to pieces you will have friends that destroy you to pieces however it is those that help you put those pieces back together that are the ones that stay in your life forever. It's those people that teach you the lessons that they've learned and help you along the way I just hope that I can guide you to the best of my ability and not let you down. You're one of my favorites and this is the only time I'm going to say it but you are one of my favorites and I do care about you deeply and love you to pieces."

I finished reading that and the waterworks came out. It was more than just a nice text for me. It was validation. Which is something I struggled with for the longest time. I always feel like I'm always asking "How are you?" and nobody ever asked me. This was confirmation. This told me that I was a good person and that I'm surrounded by beautiful people and beautiful people don't just happen.

Chapter 9 ME, FROM THE INSIDE OUT

Now that I'm healed, now that all the pieces are but in place, I want to really look back at how I got here. So, Where did it all go wrong?

My first true heartbreak was when I was in an abusive relationship. Going through something like that for anyone is hard but especially dealing with it at a young age, it can really tear you apart. I realize now that this was when the struggle with validation really started. I recognized the moments where I should've left. I should've walked out when I could've. Why did I stay? I think when you're young, you can't decide on making the right decision. Domestic violence is huge in teenage relationships. I met a lot of girls who have either been in an abusive relationship or know someone that has.

At the time I felt like I was the only one. I was scared and young, I never saw it coming. My soul for a while was running on a path that wasn't meant for me. Dealing with this and teenage hormones, I thought the world was ending. It was hard to come out from it and when I thought it was all over, the side effects still carried on. It wasn't until I opened my heart to God, I realized that he's the only one who can judge me. His love is all I need.

When I finally let go of that time in my life, it freed my soul. I could breathe again, I could love again. It took me almost two years to realize that I struggled with validation. Which lead me to the worst heartbreak of them all. The day my aunt left. I never saw that coming either. Is that why it hurt so bad or was it because of an internal struggle with myself?

My aunt was my best friend. I trusted her with a lot especially during the time of my depression. She saw sides of me I had never shared with anyone. The sides that felt like life wasn't worth living. She saw that I never recovered from all the tragedies in my life. She knew that it wasn't healthy. I never really opened up to anyone like the way I opened up to her. She's family so I thought it was safe, I thought she would always be around.

I put a lot on her. I looked to her for all the answers. She has been through alot in her lifetime and I looked up to the person she became despite of it all. I guess in most way I relied on her to breathe for me. Which isn't healthy. I had to learn that no one is gonna breathe for me. Losing my aunt was unbelievably hard. It wasn't like losing a friend, I lost family.

I've had a lot of people walk out of my life. Whether they couldn't handle the state I was in or it was there own issues, so many people have walked out. At a young age, losing people like that is hard especially when some of them were family. People will always be coming in and out of life and that's a hard lesson to learn. For a while, I didn't accept it.

It was the leaving that was hard, It was the aftermath. It's dealing with that loss amongst all the other things life throws at you. It was frustrating to miss my aunt because there was nothing I could do about it. It felt like she had passed but because she was still alive, still walking this earth, it made it harder to deal with. I guess one day or rather the day of my accident, that all changed.

I don't know if it was because of the accident or if it was because after missing her for so long, I eventually stopped missing her. My heart was no longer in that place. I cared about her but I just no longer missed her. I let go of her and I start to breathe on my own.

If this is what she wanted for me, there's a million more ways that she could've went about it. For now, I'll let God decide whether or not, I let her back into my life in the future. I will always pray for her and one day I hope that our paths cross. I appreciate all that she's helped me with. Most people would've been different but I look at it as, even with all the things she has said to me, she is family and that will never change. I guess that when you know you've really healed, when you can forgive someone who's not even sorry. I forgive her and now I've let go of the past us.

When it comes to the passing of a loved one, it's never easy. Sometimes it's expected and sometimes it's not, either way it's not easy. Losing three people in the matter of months taught me a lot. Life is a privilege, not a guarantee. It tore me apart watching people fall one by one. Death has always been a touchy subject for me, for that reason. Now since God is in my life, I'm not scared.

Maybe that's where I went wrong. I had never truly accepted God into my heart. Alll the time that I spent doubting him, I should've spent serving him. The day I started being a true follower of God is the day I stopped feeling that overwhelming feeling of pain. The day I let God in is the day I let go of my depression. I can't explain that feeling but I can show how much it has affected me.

My heart has now been flipped. I looked at love from a different point of view. Love is love in all it forms and impurities. The way I love and the way I live may be completely different from how somebody else chooses to do so. I've always been a giver. I give all I have to every person I meet because I feel that everyone should be loved. Everyone should know what it feels like to have someone that cares about them.

I always check up on people. It takes seconds out of my day,only seconds. Within those few seconds I'm influencing that person's day and their mood. That has become my lifestyle. If I can make somebody's day, If I can save a life, I'm going to, not because I get something from it but because I've been there. I know what that feels like.

God saved my life along time ago. Ever since then I've been searching for ways to improve the life of others. This world is cruel and tragedies occur everyday. Through all my searching I've met the most amazing people. It has become a passion for me, finding people who need help.

That's when I knew I was back because that change the world perspective was back. When I finally made this breakthrough I wanted to share it with the world. Every day I wake up and I am thankful. For some people they wake up and that's the hardest part of their day. It's taking that first step. If there's anything I could take away from that time in my life is that taking that step may be the best thing i've ever done.

When I give back, when I see that my efforts have succeeded, it fixes all that was ever broken in my heart and soul. It was like repairing a car after an accident, once you hear that engine rub again, there's no telling where it'll go.

Now, I look forward to seeing the sun rise in the morning. I look forward to all the beautiful lessons tomorrow holds. I wouldn't change anything that has happened on my journey. I wouldn't have done anything differently because it has led me to who I am. It has showed me the true meanings of strength, love, and faith.

I have a lot of people who look up to me. My little brothers, My second grade religion class, and all of the kids I mentor, they look up to me but little do they know I look up to them. They're all a crucial part of my recovery. If there was anything I could change, it would be that I met them all sooner. If only I decided to teach earlier.

God has had a plan for me all along. He has a reason for everything he does and I believe that with every part of me. He has given me so much even when at time I really didn't deserve it. I will always look up to the sky whenever I accomplish something because I know that I couldn't have done it without God and all of my guardian angels.

When I was a freshman, I had this group of friends. We all went through our own battles during our time together and every time they were hurting I would write them a really long letter and to the best of my ability, I would try to cheer them up. I would tell them how important they're and I would try to make sense of whatever it was they were going through even when I didn't understand it myself.

I was extremely close with them and me writing those letters was my way of showing that I appreciate them. They did lot for me and through those letters I showed my gratitude. There's one friend I had never written a letter to. He saved my life and now it's time to show my gratitude.

Dear God,

Acknowledgements

First and foremost I want to thank God for saving my life and for all the blessings he has given me. He has been my rock and the reason that I am standing here today.

Coach was the first to have any knowledge of my book and because of her I was able to keep writing. Her undying passion for the sport of hockey has inspired and motivated me in every aspect of my life. The life lessons she has taught me will always stay with me. I can't thank her enough for being my lighthouse at a time when darkness was surrounding me. The person she is today has influenced me in more ways than she could ever imagine. She's my hero for the fact that when all odds are against her she pushes till the end. She strives for greatness even when things aren't going well for her in other areas in her life. Her strength and integrity shows in the person she is today.

My aunt was the first person I shared my writing with. She was there at a time when many people weren't and so for that I am eternally grateful. She walked into my life when I needed a mentor and most importantly a friend and she did all those things well. She has helped me through numerous things and has taught me a lot during the time we spent together. She is a beautiful soul and will always have a place in my heart. I owe her a million thank yous to say the least.

Aunt Tiny came into my life at the perfect time. She has been a great influence on my life. I had told her about my book early on and she has supported me ever since. My gratitude for her can't be expressed in words. She is one of the greatest people I have ever met.

Coach B. has always been a father figure in my life. He has shown me what it really means to have a giving heart. He has been there for me since the first day we met. He's done so much for me especially through hockey. His acts of kindness will stay with me till the day I die. He has given me the gift of hockey and that's all I could ask for.

My stepmom and Dad have done more than enough for me. Dad, your wise words couldn't have come at a better time in my life, they encouraged me to move forward. I am thankful for the relationship I now have with him. My stepmom is my best friend, I thank her for always listening to my problems and cheering me up. I love the both of them with all of my heart.

My mom has always been the strong female woman in my life. She has dealt with a lot in her lifetime and she still turned out to be a great mother. She has shown me that love is love in all its forms. She has been my shoulder to cry on and just about the best mother I could ever ask for. My grandparents are the most amazing, caring, and giving people in my life and they have become like second parents to me.

My siblings have given me the greatest joys in life. For being strong leaders and little givers. I am thankful to have had them at a time when I thought I had nothing. I thank them for the love they have given me.

My God family has loved me no matter what and has showed me the grace of God. My Godfather is one of the most important people in my life and I thank him for supporting me and my book. His family's dedication to God is inspiring and I hope to follow in their footsteps.

My stepmoms side of the family along with my entire family and all those who have become family, the support you have given me is appreciated and it goes both ways. Thank you for teaching me the true meaning of family. I love each and everyone of you.

Mrs. Milano is the greatest teacher I have ever met. She has showed me kindness and love and has become such a huge part of my life. She has supported me in both the good and bad times of my life. I can't thank her enough for always being more than just a teacher.

Last but definitely not least I want to thank the kids I have met in the third period art and tech class and my second graders. Thank you all for opening my eyes but more importantly my heart. I carry your stories with me everyday and you have changed my perspective on life. My inspiration for this book is all of you.